The Hasidic Moses

The Hasidic Moses

A Chapter in the History of Jewish Interpretation

Aryeh Wineman

PICKWICK *Publications* · Eugene, Oregon

THE HASIDIC MOSES
A Chapter in the History of Jewish Interpretation

Pickwick Publications
An Imprint of Wipf and Stock Publishers
199 W. 8th Ave., Suite 3
Eugene, OR 97401

www.wipfandstock.com

PAPERBACK ISBN: 978-1-5326-5134-2
HARDCOVER ISBN: 978-1-5326-5135-9
EBOOK ISBN: 978-1-5326-5136-6

Cataloguing-in-Publication data:

Names: Wineman, Aryeh, author.

Title: The Hasidic Moses : a chapter in the history of Jewish interpretation / Aryeh Wineman.

Description: Eugene, OR: Pickwick Publications, 2018 | Includes bibliographical references.

Identifiers: ISBN 978-1-5326-5134-2 (paperback) | ISBN 978-1-5326-5135-9 (hardcover) | ISBN 978-1-5326-5136-6 (ebook)

Subjects: LCSH: Hasidim—Biblical interpretation | Moses (Biblical leader) | Bible. Pentateuch—Criticism, interpretation, etc., Jewish | Mysticism—Judaism—History | Cabala—History

Classification: BS571 W46 2018 (paperback) | BS571 (ebook)

Manufactured in the U.S.A.   02/14/19

Several chapters of this book are revisions of articles which originally appeared either in *Conservative Judaism* or in *Hebrew Studies*, the annual of the National Association of Professors of Hebrew. They appear in this volume with the permission of the respective publications.

The translations from the Hebrew Bible are my own; translation of two verses from the New Testament are taken from the *Revised Standard New Testament* (Thomas Nelson & Sons (Toronto-New York-Edinburgh, 1946).

In memory of Huston Smith

Contents

Abbreviations

b.	Babylonian Talmud
Baba Bat.	*Baba batra*
Ber.	*B'rakhot*
Cor	Corinthians
Deut	Deuteronomy
Eccl	Ecclesiastes (*Kohelet*)
Erub.	*'Erubin*
Exod	Exodus
Gen	Genesis
Hag.	*Ḥagigah*
Isa	Isaiah
j.	Jerusalem Talmud
Jer	Jeremiah
Kidd.	*Kiddushin*
Lev	Leviticus
m.	Mishna
m. Abot	Mishna *Avot*
Meh.	*M'khilta d'Rabbi Yishma'el*
Midr. Deut.	*Midrash D'varim rabbah*

Midr. Eccl.	*Midrash Kohelet rabbah*
Midr. Exod.	*Midrash Sh'mot rabbah*
Midr. Gen.	*Midrash B'reshit rabbah*
Midr. Lam.	*Midrash Ekha rabbah*
Midr. Lev.	*Midrash Vayikra rabbah*
Midr. Num.	*Midrash B'midbar rabbah*
Midr. Shir	*Midrash Shir ha-shirim rabbah*
Matt	Mathew
Ned.	*N'darim*
Num	*B'midbar*
Pesah.	*P'sahim*
Pesiq. Rab Kah.	*P'sikta d'rav Kahana*
Pirque R. El.	*Pirke deRabbi Eliezer*
Prov	Proverbs
Ps / Pss	Psalm(s)
Rosh.	*Rosh ha-shanah*
Sabb.	*Shabbat*
Sanh.	*Sanhedrin*
Sipre	*Sifre*
Song	Song of Songs (*Shir ha-shirim*)
Sukk.	*Sukkah*
Tanh.	*Midrash Tanḥuma*
Yalqut	*Yalkut Shim'oni*
Zach.	Zachariah

Note: The Midrash on the Five Books of Moses (Genesis, Exodus, Leviticus, Numbers, and Deuteronomy) and the Five Scrolls (Song of Songs, Ruth, Lamentations, Ecclesiastes, and Esther) are collected and printed in *Midrash rabbah*.

1

Prelude
An Itinerary

An account of any person, from any point-in-time, is never a finished product. Rather such a story continues and grows from one generation to another and from one era to another. It comes to mirror new sensitivities which come to the fore along the path of time.

In Jewish tradition, the meaning of the scriptural text is not bounded by the text itself. The past is retold in a way to serve as a source and treasure of later insight. A narrative set in the past takes on new life from generation to generation. This is, perhaps, the broadest definition of the phenomenon of *midrash* as a later generation's reading an older text in light of its own experience, values, and sensitivities. The initial account, even when set down in a written text, is never the last and final word, and a personage of the past is re-conceived over time as that person becomes the subject of re-telling.

In the Torah, Moses is associated with the Exodus from slavery in ancient Egypt and also with the Revelation at Sinai as well as with the trials of his leadership both leading up to the departure from Egypt and the years of wandering in the desert. He is given a considerable life-span but dies before being allowed to complete his task. In rabbinic lore, intensifying the sense of the biblical text, Moses pleads to live on and experience a sense of fulfillment of his life's endeavor, but that privilege and satisfaction is denied him. Though he argues and pleads to live on, employing every means and argument at his command and imagination, his pleading is nevertheless rejected and he dies.

As he is viewed through various universes of discourse, the narrative concerning Moses is ceaselessly expanded and deepened through time along with the very conception of who and what Moses was. His life comes to mirror concepts and values of later eras, and he outgrows even the limitations of his biblical life-span. He is given the highest praise, and he is also the recipient of profound criticism.

In the chapters that follow, we will note how the Eastern European commentators and preachers of Hasidic teaching, primarily in the eighteenth and early nineteenth centuries, recast the account of Moses in the light of their own image and emphases and world-view. We will begin with an introduction to the terrain and landscape of the subject by a discussion of the very character of Hasidic interpretation of the Torah. This will be followed by viewing various excerpts and examples in which the Hasidic Masters, in quite diverse ways, creatively elaborated upon what is told about the life of Moses in the Torah-text in a way to express themes and values basic to Hasidism's message and self-image. While pointing in various directions, each of these excerpts from a range of homily-texts re-creates the biblical account of Moses in some noteworthy and interesting respects.

Then we will explore how the Hasidic preachers creatively re-conceived the two major themes so central in the biblical account of Moses—the Exodus from Egypt and the Revelation-scene at Mount Sinai—and will become acquainted with a significant Hasidic statement of the role of interpretation through time. Our journey will bring us to a surprising explanation of Moses' death in a way that both envisions his soul's return to the world throughout the generations, along with statements of criticism of what some

Hasidic thinkers understood as Moses' own intentions had he been able to enter the Land with his people. Then, turning to Moses' role as a lawgiver—or, more precisely, as an agent of Divine Revelation of a body of law—we will examine how the Hasidic homilists related to the laws involving the biblical priestly cult centered around the sacrificial altar. And journeying still further, we will explore the various ways that the Hasidic thinkers conceived of Moses himself in terms of who and what he was—or is—stretching from grasping Moses as a person bounded by time and a human life-span to his more essential metaphorical role which transcends time itself.

Every age shares in an innate tendency to grasp the past in terms of its own hour of history and its own mentality, values, and experience, and the Hasidic stream that emerged in eighteenth-century Eastern Europe was no exception.

An acquaintance with the basic literary expressions of Hasidic teaching in its earlier period, the classic homily-texts, point to the presence of a highly creative process of interpretation of traditional and sacred texts. The revered texts of Jewish tradition are largely read on a metaphorical level colored by a mode of spirituality that often radically re-created or added to their earlier meaning. In fact, what stands out from an acquaintance with these homily-texts might precisely be their remarkable creativity. The reader is invited to participate in a journey that recasts both the biblical Moses and the central themes associated with Moses in Jewish tradition to comprise an inexhaustible source of ongoing spiritual insight.

The late Jewish literary scholar, Shalom Spiegel, would refer to the "afterlife of the Bible," by which he meant that its narratives, concepts, and laws, and even the wording of the text continued to have a life of their own, which reflects the growing wisdom, experience, and insight of many later generations. In Jewish tradition the words of the Hebrew Bible were explored and analyzed in a way to serve as a source of ever-new ideas and interpretations, and its stories gave birth to new stories and narrative variations that spoke to a later time-period, serving as a garment for significant insights making their appearance over time.

The role and scenario of the biblical Moses was, in various degrees, re-created in many different eras, and the re-creation of the biblical Moses at the hands of Hasidic preachers and commentators contributed to the ongoing re-telling of his life and the re-shaping of his very identity in a way that spoke meaningfully to them, to their own following, and their own time, and which might relate to the deeper spiritual quest of our own hour of history as well.

Welcome to the journey!

2

How the Hasidic Masters
Read the Torah[1]

THE NATURE OF THE HASIDIC HOMILY

To understand a plant, it is necessary to consider the soil in which it is situated. The plant—or trans-plant—in this analogy is Moses himself, the figure Moses as understood in biblical and also rabbinic texts. The soil in our analogy is the very character of classical Hasidic interpretation, which casts light on how the early teachers and preachers of the Hasidic stream re-created, in some significant and highly interesting ways, not only the figure and life-story of Moses, which they received from earlier generations, but virtually every element of the sacred texts and the tradition they inherited.

The collections of homilies from Hasidism's classical period—from the latter decades of the eighteenth through the early decades of the nineteenth century—have been mined and continue to be mined as a source of Hasidic teaching, in fact, as the major source

1. An earlier version of this chapter appeared in *Conservative Judaism* 60.1–2 (2007–8) 62–73.

of Hasidic thought in that early period. With rare exception, the Hasidic world-view and its ideas were not presented at all systematically as an organized body of concepts. They were communicated rather in the form of sermonic discussions on the weekly Torah-portions, a highly traditional form and medium, even when the content of those same homilies might comprise a radically innovative understanding of the traditional texts themselves.

This same body of sermonic notes can be approached as a highly creative reading of the Torah, the basic Jewish sacred text. Doing so calls for focusing not solely on the idea-content of the homilies, but also on how any particular Hasidic master and homilist made the journey from A to B, the sometimes seemingly galactic journey from the plain meaning (*p'shat*) of the hallowed Torah-text to his own interpretation significantly removed from the more conventional and evident understanding of the same text. Beyond its role as a vehicle of communication, the Hasidic homily reveals how the Torah-text lived within the consciousness of the Hasidic masters and what they heard or overheard in it. The meanings derived from biblical verses go much beyond the earlier, more systematic and formal medieval conception of four levels of meaning in their addressing primarily the inner life. Certain traits, qualities, and premises account for the pronounced transformation of the meaning and even of the texture of the Torah-text as grasped in the Hasidic homily in a way that might have a very contemporary appeal.

A FOCUS ON THE INNER DIMENSION

While inheriting traditions of interpretation from earlier periods, the Hasidic Masters also interpreted a passage or verse from the Torah in the context of their own specific value-complex. And perhaps the single core-value around which that complex revolved is *p'nimi'ut*—innerness itself, the inner being and depth-dimension of the self, of the Torah, of existence, and even of God. Whatever the actual or more evident nature of the Torah-text that he expounded, the Hasidic preacher grasped the ultimate setting of the specific passage to be the Jew's inner life as it confronts both the complexity of the human make-up and the unique soulfulness found at the deepest level of a person's psyche.

In this light, a number of Hasidic Masters read God's initial command to Avram, *leikh l'kha* ("Go forth," Gen 12:2) in light of the idiom's two words read literally and separately as "Go/to you." Kalonymus Kalman Epstein of Krakow, for example, read that expression as a call addressed to every person to penetrate beyond the more external aspects of the self to one's truer, deeper, and innermost self, which he identified as an aspect and expression of the Divine.[2] The same is true of the identification, in some Hasidic homilies, of *'Amalek*—the heartless foe who attacked the weak and defenseless Hebrews on their trek through the desert and who is to be blotted out—not as any particular tribe or population, whether identifiable or not, but rather as the Evil Inclination within the self of every person.[3] What in the Torah-text would appear to relate to what is "out there" is read as an allusion to what is *within*.[4]

In one of his homilies, Menahem Nahum of Chernobyl related to words in the Torah that introduce regulations concerning the burnt-offering (*torat ha'olah*, Lev 6:1–2), explaining that verse in terms of a person's need to subdue the Evil Inclination (*yeitzer hara*). The homilist proceeded to explain *torat ha'olah*—the offering that is almost completely burnt on the altar and ascends in smoke—as "the Torah of ascent," in that by means of the Torah, properly studied, a person might be able to *ascend* to a higher level. And drawing upon an intertextual link with Jacob's night of wrestling with "the man" all night until the break of dawn (Gen 32:25), the preacher went on to grasp the following verse, "The burnt offering itself shall remain just where it is burned upon the altar all night until morning . . ." (Lev 6:2), in that "a person can raise up the darkness within himself and transform it into the light of the morning."[5]

2. *Ma'or va-shemesh*, I, 8b–9a.

3. *No'am Elimelekh*, 148 (*B'shalaḥ*).

4. Note Margolin, *Mikdash adam*, 115–17.

5. *Ma'or 'einayim*, 43ab (*Tzav*).

The reader notes that the homily includes no mention whatsoever of the actual subject of the Torah-passage, namely the burnt-offering and the procedure connected with that sacrificial offering, but instead ponders the transforming function of Torah-study in subduing the Evil Inclination (*yeitzer hara*) within one's makeup. While the Torah-text focuses directly on the details of how a particular type of sacrificial offering is to be offered, the homilist overheard in those same verses something quite different, namely an *inner* transformation, a happening and a drama that take place not upon the altar but within a person's own inner self.

The Hasidic homily, as evident in the above example, is often emphatically psychological—without the preacher ever having read Freud or Jung—and introspective. Its frequent translation of various types of passages from the Torah to a specifically internal plane is likely enticing to the contemporary preacher and the modern student of Torah as it substitutes for considerations of historical context and historicity, with all the questions raised in connection with them, a focus on psychological insight and reads the Torah-passage as an existential observation of human life, emotions, conflicts, and growth in spiritual awareness.

The homily cited above, we might add, has a distinctly prayerful character. And furthermore, any passage from the Torah, irrespective of subject-matter, when sifted through the interpretative process of the Hasidic homily, tends to acquire that kind of devotional character. This "character-change" in the texture of the Torah-text suggests an implicit understanding, to the homilist's mind, that the tone of his homily reflects the real nature of the Torah-text itself, and furthermore that the Torah in its entirety and in its every word is devotional in character as it addresses a person's inner life and the way to serve and worship God in the deepest and most comprehensive sense. The homily grasps the Torah-passage in a way that it might touch a deeper level of the self where it aims to transform the person.

TRANSCENDING TIME AND CONTEXT

That inner-directed bent in the Hasidic homily impacts a clear tendency of "parabolization," the strategy of reading biblical happenings in a way to elicit a metaphorical function relating to the devotee's own spiritual life and struggles.[6] What an account in the Torah presents as specific moments of the past become, in the homily, archetypal events that might radiate every person's life at any time.[7] What is written in the past tense in the Torah-text is read, in effect, as a narrative that is constantly recurring.

The early Hasidic homilists regarded *p'shat* (the literal, surface meaning of the text) with its natural focus on one-time happenings as largely irrelevant to a text's more significant meaning. They viewed *p'shat* as corresponding to the lowest dimension of the soul and as the "garment" of the more inner teaching identified as the real meaning of the text.[8] Without explicitly negating the *p'shat,* they tended to view occurrences that happen "out there" including the "stuff of history" and also the "stuff of narrative" as quite beside the point. Words that in the Torah have a precise context in the life of a particular individual or even of the sacred history of the people of Israel are read, in the Hasidic homily, to apply to every person at any time, just as God's initial call to Abraham was read as a perpetually recurrent call addressed to every person in every era, and as the Pharaoh of the Exodus-tradition is said to refer to any person of any time who is given to stubborn behavior and attitudes.[9]

In *Tol'dot Ya'akov Yosef,* the very first printed Hasidic text, the preacher of Polonnoye repeatedly posed the question concerning any episode or law in the Torah: what is the import of that verse, detail, episode, or law in relation to any and every person and time? The Torah, in his view, is not a record of past happenings or of laws that are, in certain eras, inapplicable. The true meaning of

6. Ricoeur, "The Bible and the Imagination," 52.
7. Scholem, *Major Trends*, 19.
8. *Degel maḥane Efrayim*, 266 (*Ha'azinu*).
9. *Tol'dot Ya'akov Yosef*, I, 146 (*Bo*).

any element in the Torah—it is presumed—must have validity and relevance concerning *all* persons and *all* times.

This trait is exemplified, for example, in a Hasidic reading of the episode of Rebecca's unbearable pain during her pregnancy, as she is told that she bears within her womb two nations engaged in conflict (Gen 25:22). In the eyes of the Hasidic homilist, the particular physical difficulties of one particular person long ago—even if she be one of the biblical matriarchs—would be of questionable relevance. And so Efrayim of Sedilikov read that episode in a way that relates not to one particular woman in pain but rather to every person in every time, male or female, reading it as a drama occurring within the self of each person, a conflict between the good inclination and the more deeply-rooted evil inclination within the human makeup.[10] Similarly the war that God wished to spare the unprepared Israelites must be understood, according to Yitzhak of Radvil, not in terms of a specific crisis confronting the generation of Israelites in the wilderness, but rather as a recurrent temptation, present at all times, to "return to Egypt"—to turn to those values which comprise the very antithesis of holiness.[11]

More generally, passages that, in the Torah, relate to a particular person or situation tend to be read in the Hasidic homily in a way that relates to what is significantly more universal. We find in the Torah the verse, "And (the rite of Yom Kippur) shall atone for the Israelites from all their sins *once a year (ahat bashanah)*" (Lev 16:34), a verse that concludes the Torah's prescription of cultic practices for the Day of Atonement. To the ear and mind of Efrayim of Sedilikov, however, the word *shanah* ("year") alludes to the verb-root *shno* ("study") as he ascribed to Torah-study with pure intent the power to atone for one's sins. He furthermore read the word *ahat* ("one, once") as the kind of devotional spirit that brings the *One*, the Master of the Universe, within one's very act of study.[12] Through this kind of word-play in Efrayim's homily, words relating to a rite occurring explicitly but once a year are read to

10. *Degel*, 34–35 (*Tol'dot*).

11. *Or Yitzhak*, 117 (*B'shalah*).

12. *Degel*, (*Ahare mot*), 175.

apply to every day of the year. A biblical verse might be understood in various ways, but its most relevant meaning, the homilist assumes, is one that applies to all time, not exclusively to a single point-of-time in the past or limited to a specific day during the course of the year.

A striking example of such transformation becomes evident in another comment upon a cultic passage in the Torah. The purification ritual for those rendered ritually impure through their contact with a corpse, the rite involving a red heifer, is referred to in the Torah as *ḥukkat ha-torah* ("a statute of the Torah," Num 19:2), the word (*ḥok*) suggesting laws that do not lend themselves to rational understanding. That differentiation between laws that can and cannot be understood and explained by the intellect, however, suggested to Menahem Nahum of Chernobyl another differentiation, one distinguishing the revealed form of the Torah, to which one can apply the human intellect, from the light within the Torah that has a transformative effect even though in itself it is situated beyond the reach of the human mind. A person engaging in Torah with pure and unselfish motivation can transform himself through attaching his own *ḥiyyut* ("life-vitality") to that light present within the Torah, a light that one can experience but never truly understand, "the flowing light from which the Torah is carved."[13]

Not only is *Mitzrayim* ("Egypt") understood metaphorically not as a specific locality or region or regime but rather as futile worldly pursuits or as the force of ego and inner enslavement and the failure to realize the presence of the Divine in all that is, but even the basic symbolic foods of the *Pesaḥ* festival are explained in a way that is quite independent of the context of the Exodus-narrative. *Yitzḥak* of Radvil explained the command to eat unleavened bread as due to its lack of taste: the eating of *matza* indicates that the Israelites correctly looked to food as a means of sustaining the body in life rather than as a way to satisfy physical desires or cravings, which can comprise a kind of idolatry.[14] And earlier, Ya'akov

13. *Ma'or 'einayim* (*Ḥukkat*), 52b–53a.
14. *Or Yitzḥak* (*Bo*), 112–13.

Yosef of Polonnoye explained *matza* as "the bread of humility" in contrast with leavened bread (*ḥametz*) which, rising up, suggests haughtiness, arrogance, and egotism. The need for inspection of *matza* as it is baking then translates into the need to insure that even our humility not contain some particle of pride or ego. The Polonnoye preacher also explained the eating of *maror* (bitter herbs) at the *Pesaḥ Seder* in terms not of Egyptian oppression but rather of the place of bitterness—experiences of disappointment and seemingly needless struggle—in the economy of life: one's desirous and egotistical tendencies are so strong that a person can prevail over them only through the measure of bitterness and disappointment that we meet in life.[15]

This trait of reading biblical passages in a way that transcends time and context might have appeal to any contemporary reader who recoils from a fundamentalist mentality and reading of a scriptural text. Without necessarily negating *p'shat* (the literal, surface meaning of a text), the mode of Hasidic interpretation tends to locate the more significant meaning of any toraitic passage elsewhere. In this, it follows in the path of earlier kabbalistic teaching[16] but in its own more distinct manner which largely substitutes its accent on interiority for Kabbalah's elaborate theosophical myth. The classical Hasidic homilist grasped the Torah as a network of allusions which one hears—or overhears—in the text.[17] The Hasidic Masters read the sacred text of the Torah, in effect, less as prose, transmitting details, than as poetry which similarly speaks in a language of allusion. They approached the Torah-text—one might further suggest—much like a melody the real significance of which is to be found on the level of its overtones.

15. *Tol'dot* Ya'akov Yosef (*Bo*), I, 167.

16. Note Idel, *Kabbalah—New Perspectives*, 200–249 and *Absorbing Perfections*, 137–63.

17. *Or Yitzḥak* (*B'shalaḥ*), 117; also (*Yitro*), 126.

THE INNER, SUBLIME, PRIMORDIAL TORAH

Bound up with the Hasidic homily's rationale for its innovative interpretation is a fundamental premise. Menahem Nahum of Chernobyl, as quoted above, referred to "the flowing light from which the Torah is carved." To the Hasidic master and homilist, the *p'shat* (plain, surface meaning) of the Torah is not its ultimate statement; rather, like a human being, the Torah too is considered as having both a visible body and an inner, deeper aspect quite beyond the reach either of our senses or of our minds. The Torah as we recognize it, a document composed of letters and words relating to human existence in this physical reality with a focus on physical behavior and deeds, is said to be a garment (*malbush*) of the more ultimate and sublime state of the Torah that preceded the coming into being of material reality.[18]

The Hasidic Masters viewed the Torah as we are familiar with it to be a translation of that higher state of the Torah to our own level of being in order to accommodate our limitations and our own physical reality. With all the reverence due it as our indispensable channel to connect with its higher dimensions, the Torah as spelled out in language, law, and narrative-account nevertheless ultimately remains a garment. That recognition, a truly radical aspect of the consciousness of the Hasidic master, understandably served as a significant element in his exercising such license in going beyond the surface meaning and striving to read the text of the Torah as a network of allusions and overtones suggesting a deeper and more inner meaning.

Yehudah Aryeh Lev Alter of Gur (1847–1905), a later Hasidic master who both echoed and distilled some of the core-emphases of Hasidism's classical period, taught that

> . . . the Torah as we know it is the garb (*malbush*) of the Torah in its higher state, and through one's engaging in the (study of) the Torah in its revealed and external state, the power of its innerness awakens. The very essence of

---

18. See *Midr. Gen.*, 17.5, also Heschel, *God in Search of Man*, 262–63, and Scholem, *On the Kabbalah and its Symbolism*, 41–50.

the capacity given to the people of Israel is the ability to awaken the (higher) source of the Torah . . . . Through our effort, the power of the Torah's interiority infuses . . . the garb, and the covering becomes attached to its inner core . . . ."[19]

In that thought, Yehuda Aryeh Lev of Gur perhaps defined the ultimate aspiration of the classical Hasidic homily. At its best, it sought to connect the Torah in its concrete sense and form with its higher, sublime roots. It aspired to understand the garb in a way that its Divine interior impacts, permeates, and radiates it. In his study and expounding of Torah, the Hasidic master aspired to experience and allude to something of the "flowing light from which the Torah is carved," and to understand the garment itself in the light of that more sublime source.

AFTERTHOUGHT: THE GULF AND THE BRIDGE

Two centuries after Hasidism's classical period, Jews influenced by modern biblical studies necessarily view the Torah through a very different lens, one that accentuates precisely time and historic background and context. Hence, with the quest for historical understanding, the Torah-text is approached as a document rooted in ancient Near Eastern culture and sharing, to a certain degree, the practices and beliefs of that world, even when it sometimes transcends that background in remarkable and highly significant ways. In relating to the Torah as an historical document, modern biblical scholarship seeks to define the meaning of that text in terms of what it could mean at the time and place of its emergence and development. And in doing so, biblical criticism also restores an exclusive focus on the *p'shat*, as other traditional levels of meaning are deemed irrelevant, after-the-fact, distinctly foreign to the Torah's own time and cultural background.

---

19. *S'fat emet*, IV, 1877, 3b.

Intellectual honesty, in fact, directs us to understand the Torah, in that sense, as an historical document with roots in a specific time, place, and background. At the same time, in its larger religious meaning, however, Torah assumes a very different character. In the latter sense, the Torah is not circumscribed by the spiritual or intellectual boundaries of ancient Israel and the ancient Near East. It is rather a text that has assumed a life of its own, giving rise to new meanings through time; it is the Torah of rabbinic midrash and of Kabbalah and of the Hasidic homily and of interpretation reflecting also our own hour of time with its questions and sensitivities and consciousness. The Torah, in this sense, is open to new and expanded meaning over time and is not limited or bounded by the text's potential meaning at the time of its emergence.

Approaching the Torah as a text having a life of its own might suggest that in its ultimate, more sublime sense, the Torah is not only more than the product of a particular period of history but that furthermore its meaning is never fully realized in any period, that the higher reaches of Torah are beyond time and beyond words. As Rabbi Nahman of Bratslav would emphasize,[20] there is need to go beyond the words themselves to refract its higher Roots, that infinite aspect of Torah that is clad, but never fully expressed, in that document that we revere.

If the Maggid of Mezhirech and his students saw in the concrete historic and linguistic form of the Torah a *translation* to our own finite physical reality of what is itself sublime, transcendent and infinite,[21] we in our day might expand upon that model to perceive in the concrete form and content of the Torah a translation of that higher, infinite sense of Torah to the language, experience, and mentality of a particular time, place, and cultural background. The concrete Torah that we read is then understood as an historic expression, with its inherent time-bound limitations, of a Divine

---

20. *Ḥayyei Moharan*, part 2 (*Shivḥei Moharan*), *G'dulat hasagato*, #47, 16. Also Heschel (*Ibid.* 262, 274–76).

21. *Maggid d'varav leYa'akov*, homilies #56, #122, #134.

wisdom and insight that itself transcends all historical periods and expressions and radiates all of them.[22]

22. Heschel, *God in Search of Man*, also Green, *See My Face, Speak My Name*, and Wineman, "Hewn from the Divine Quarry."

3

Hasidic Re-creation of the Biblical Account of Moses

The following is a rather partial sampling of excerpts from classical Hasidic texts that interpret aspects of the biblical account of Moses or of his endeavors in ways that spotlight various Hasidic themes and values, reading the Hasidic value-complex into—or sometimes: out of—the biblical text and narrative themselves. The excerpts are taken largely from various collections of sermonic comments on those parts of the Torah-text that comprise the biblical Moses-narrative.

AT MOSES' BIRTH

"And the woman conceived and she bore a son, and she saw that he is good . . ." (Exod 2:1) "Yocheved knew that her son was good (*tov*), for she saw the Hidden Light with him. At his birth, Moses merited that light due to his soul's exceedingly high stature." [*Maor 'einayim, Sh'mot,* 31ab]

Comment: Menahem Nahum of Chernobyl read in the word *tov* (good) something exceedingly unusual and holy which Moses' mother perceived at her younger son's very birth. Her son is viewed here

17

as being emphatically different from other infants, even from his very first moments in life. Rashi, referring to a talmudic comment (*b. Sotah* 12a), explained that at Moses' birth, the house became filled with light, a comment found also in *Midr. Exod.*, 1:24. The reader might immediately recognize a parallel, to a degree, with the account of the appearance of an exceedingly bright star in the sky with the birth of Jesus (Matt 2:1–2) and also with a tradition that Abraham was born in a cave which suddenly turned into a scene of highly unusual brightness (Ginzberg, *Legends*, I, 188, with sources listed in V, 209, n. 13). In addition, it was said that at Abraham's birth a bright star appeared in the eastern sky that then swallowed four other stars. (Ginzberg, *Legends*, II, 207–9, with note 48 in V, 216). Such stories might well reflect the influence of Zoroastrian lore with its accent upon light and/or the association of the face of the Assyrian deity displaying a brilliant brightness.

Perhaps in the wake of a comment in the Zohar (II, 11b) referring to the light of the *Shekhinah* (Divine Presence) which appeared at the scene of Moses' birth, Menahem Nahum of Chernobyl went further to identify that light with the Hidden Light (*ha'or ha-gannuz*), a light having brightness that far exceeded that of the sun, a light that was both physical and spiritual in nature, and which is said to have been hidden after the period of Creation. In the above passage, Menahem Nahum suggested that with the birth of Moses something of that great Hidden Light was revealed. The reader can connect the comment of the Hasidic homilist with a paradoxical Hasidic theme that the primordial light, said to be so emphatically hidden already in the world's earliest days, is actually hidden in the Torah in a way that it can nevertheless be revealed.

Avraham Hayyim of Zlozetch explained that, at Moses' birth, his sister, Miriam, (also known as "Miriam the prophet") could envision that the quality of *Da'at* (spiritual knowledge and understanding) was born and had come to the world. [*Orah l'hayyim (Sh'mot)*, 101]

MOSES KILLS THE EGYPTIAN

"And it was in those days that when Moses grew up and went out to his brothers and saw their distress, he saw an Egyptian beat a Hebrew man from among his brothers. He looked all around him and saw that there is no person there and he smote the Egyptian and buried him in the sand. On the following day two Hebrew men were fighting, and he said to the wicked one, 'Why are you striking your fellow?' The man said, 'Who appointed you as an officer and judge over us? Will you kill me as you killed the Egyptian?' . . . " (Exod 2:11–13) "In every place and person the vital life-energy (*ḥiyyut*) of the Creator is present, as it is said, 'You give life to all of them' (Neh 9:6). In the case of Israelites who cleave to God, their life-quality is very central and looms large in comparison with the comparatively lesser aspect of their bodies. . . . In contrast, through one's wickedness, a person's *ḥiyyut* is lessened in comparison with his bodily desires and his arrogance and transgressions which serve to conceal and bury his own *ḥiyyut* . . . . The words, 'And the king of Egypt died' (Exod 2:23), convey that the king intensified his wickedness and his evil decrees which are called 'death' (*mitah*) insofar as, with those decrees, his very life-quality became diminished. . . .

"When the *tzaddik* (righteous person) feels disgust in a person and his wickedness, through the *tzaddik's* own attachment to the Creator he feels compassion for the *ḥiyyut*, the Divine quality imprisoned within that person. His emphatic compassion cleaves to the person's *ḥiyyut* and deplores the pronounced wickedness which surrounds it. In this way he casts that wickedness to the ground while, due to the *tzaddik's* mercy for that *ḥiyyut* (which is holy and partakes of the Name of God), the person's very life-quality cleaves and ascends to its higher Source, even while the wicked person himself falls dead. . . .

"Through the light of the *tzaddik's* countenance, Moses expelled the (impure) Shell (*k'lipah*) . . . surrounding the holy spark in the person. And as the Shell fell, the *ḥiyyut*, the person's true innerness, which had been covered over and concealed within him, is then revealed.

"This is the meaning of the expression that 'he killed him with the Ineffable Name' (the holiest name for God, a name that is never to be pronounced. See Rashi's comment on Exod 2:14). The Name which was the very life-force and quality of the Egyptian separated from his body and ascended to its Source." [*Divrat Sh'lomo* (*Sh'mot*), 34b]

Comment: In contrast with the directness and simplicity of the biblical passage itself and even of its midrashic explanations, Shlomo of Luntz viewed Moses' killing the Egyptian through the lens of a rather complicated set of ideas. The reader can easily grasp the preacher's need for such an involved explanation in his being aghast at the very thought of Moses' having killed a person, even one who dealt mercilessly with an oppressed slave. The simple language of the biblical account, he proposed, must be understood through that much more complex grasp of the nature of a human being who naturally contains a hidden core of holiness even when it is concealed and camouflaged by his own wickedness which imprisons his own higher self.

THE DESERT

"And Moses was tending the sheep of Jethro, his wife's father, a priest of Midian, and he led the sheep in the desert. . . ." (Exod 3:1) "Moses led his sheep in the direction of the desert to be alone and secluded from his household so that nothing might confuse his thinking." [*Divre Moshe* (*Sh'mot*), 167]

Comment: The desert (*midbar*, "wilderness") in these texts must be grasped against the background of its connotation in many older sources in which the *midbar* did not have particularly positive or pietistic connotations. The book of Deuteronomy speaks of the *midbar* as a place of fiery serpents (Deut 8:15) and as an "empty but exceedingly noisy wasteland" (Deut 32:10), and in the biblical Yom Kippur rite (Lev 16:8–10) the scapegoat bearing the sins of the Israelites was sent beyond the camp to the wilderness which bears the name *Azazel*, which the Babylonian Talmud (*b. Yoma* 67b) explains as "a land that is hard and rough."

The scene of the Sinai-Revelation thus appears as a kind of spiritual oasis within the brutal terrain of the wilderness, a place not really fit for human habitation. And Divine protection for the Israelites and their willingness to undergo the long journey and sojourn in the wilderness is seen against the background of the very dangerous nature of the *midbar*. When the aggadic imagination speaks of the Torah's having been given in a moment of complete silence (*Midr. Exod.*, 29.9), that silence relates to an event at a specific moment of time and not to a geographical terrain.

The Zohar, the masterpiece of Jewish mystic literature composed in the late thirteenth century, describes the desert as a place of demons and evil spirits (I, 188ab) and as the place where Solomon acquired the secrets of sorcery, associated with impurity (I, 112b). The *Sitra aḥra*, the demonic, evil force, is said to reign there in the *midbar*, and the Israelites had to cross the desert for a period of forty years in order to break its power (II. 157a). Elsewhere in the Zohar, the desert, as an inherently demonic location, is associated principally not with dryness but rather with darkness and impurity.

Bypassing such earlier associations of the desert (*midbar*) with the demonic in biblical and rabbinic sources, in the passage quoted above, Moshe ben Dan Shoham sees Moses as specifically and intentionally seeking out the desert as a place of solitude. That natural setting provided him with a location allowing for a sense of awe and wonder in a way that speaks to one's inner life without any interference from his surroundings. The solitude of the desert, the homilist felt, allows for a flawless spirituality.

The comment of Moshe of Dolina echoes a sense of the desert expressed in the writings of Bahya Ibn Pekudah, whose *Ḥovot hal'vavot* ("Duties of the Heart"), written in twelfth-century Spain, was influenced by Sufi and perhaps also Christian ascetics for whom he expressed qualified admiration. In *Ḥovot hal'vavot*, Bahya Ibn Pekuda viewed the desert and the life of seclusion and solitude as a setting that prepared Moses to receive a task directing him to a very different milieu where he would struggle to liberate his fellow Israelites.

A later figure, Bahya ben Asher, explained in his *Commentary on the Torah* (*Bei'ur latorah*) concerning Exod 3:1, that "biblical figures chose to become shepherds so as to distance themselves from sinful ways, prevalent in settled areas, and to seclude themselves in prophecy." But while inspired by those ascetics who sought a seclusion from human society, both Bahya Ibn Pekudah and Bahya ben Asher, who lived a few centuries apart in the Iberian peninsula, nevertheless rejected asceticism in itself and separation from the community as a legitimate mode of life for Jews.

"And God directed the people around along the way of the desert of the Sea of Reeds" (Exod 13:18). "For reasons of seclusion, (God) led them around through the desert, that they might experience seclusion to focus their thought on a single concern, namely, their worship." [*No'am Elimelekh* (*B'shalaḥ*), 147].

And later, **"On the third month, after the Israelites went out of Egypt, on this day they came to the desert of Sinai"** (Exod 19:1). "Desert (wilderness): an intimation of pronounced solitude (*hitbod'dut*). For there, in that setting, the *tzaddik* (the righteous person or leader) is alone where he can attach himself to God." [Ibid., 154]

"And they journeyed from *R'fidim* and came to the Desert of Sinai . . ." (Exod 19:2). "A human being includes four elements: fire, wind (spirit), water, and dust. When the force of dust predominates in a person, he becomes exceedingly lazy and retreats from Torah-study and worship. But when that person gains control of himself and awakens from his dust, he makes a determined effort in worship, and then he arrives at a higher level which is called 'the Desert of Sinai,'" [Ibid., (*Yitro*), 154]

Comment: Elimelekh of Lyzhansk, who read the collective experience of the Israelites in the desert as an experience of *hitbod'dut* (seclusion), understood Moses' personal experience in the desert as a spiritual prerequisite for that collective role in which the Israelites as a whole experienced *hitbod'dut*—a role that also exemplifies the role of the *tzaddik,* the central figure in a Hasidic community who, even as the central figure in a communal group, must also experience seclusion allowing for a deep inner attachment to God (Note *No'am Elimelekh, B'shalaḥ,* 141 and *Yitro,* 154).

In the eyes of the homilist, the journey through the desert and its terrain serves as a metaphor for a spiritual journey in which the people-at-large are able to emerge as *tzaddikim* whose lives reflect a sense and conception of holiness. And he read that journey, defined in the biblical text in geographical terms, as expressive of a spiritual journey of the human being, one understood as a possibility in every person's life wherever one lives.

"And Moses was tending the sheep . . ." (Exod 3:1). "This detail in the Torah comes to show us something of his righteousness: even though Moses our Teacher was worthy of prophecy, nevertheless he was a shepherd." [*Kol Simḥah (Sh'mot),* 17b]

Comment: While spiritually, Moses occupied a supremely high level as the human transmitter of the Divine word and law, we see him, at this point in the narrative, simply as a tender of sheep in the desert, working for his wife's father, Jethro. That detail might direct our attention not necessarily to his righteousness as to his humility, as he is employed to work on a rather simple menial level, tending a flock of sheep. With his focus on that detail, Simḥah Bunam of Parsishka made a point to distinguish one's rank in the eyes of society on the basis of the type of work in which that person is engaged from that same person's true potential that might evade the public eye.

From this digression on the theme of the wilderness/desert and Moses' employment as a shepherd, let us return to the narrative which brings the reader to the Burning Bush.

THE BURNING BUSH

"And there appeared to him an angel of the Lord in a fiery flame within a bush, and he saw and behold the bush is aflame, but the bush was not consumed" (Exod 3:2). "The bush represents the entire array of worlds which, when compared with the Higher Reality, appears small and lowly. Similarly a human being, due to his body, sees nothing of the pure and bright light of God. But the very essence of the Divine—the Life that is the Source of all life—is present even within our very flesh. There it is hidden until one accustoms himself to grasp this truth and to unclad everything of its materiality in order to cleave constantly to the life-energy (ḥiyyut) present within everything, knowing that all the worlds are as a mustard-seed in the presence of the Divine brightness and recognizing the Creator's lovingkindness which gives him life. Awe, the impulse to cleave to the great light of God, brings one to a love of God . . . . In the moment of such attachment all the worlds are then removed from their very existence. Then one can experience, even if just to a small degree, the very pleasantness of God's light which is contracted, even as one's soul almost departs . . . .

"'An angel of God' is the experience and realization of such awe. The bush becomes aflame in that one attains the level of understanding the light of God which surrounds all that exists. One's spiritual bashfulness prevents a person from seeing that Light, even as one longs all the more to see it. All the worlds together are here referred to as an angel; it is the Ineffable Name which is everywhere. There is no place without its presence.

"Moses' sin at that moment was that a person, at a moment of such utter attachment to God, must view himself as nothing (ayin), as though nothing exists, for only the Divine life-energy (ḥiyyut) truly exists . . . . God alone exists, and consequently a person's thought should be directed not to one's own pleasure and needs, nor even to a sense of delight derived from one's attachment to the light of the Infinite One. Rather, one must regard himself as non-existent and, consequently, 'God is One and His Name One'" (Zach 14:9). [Divrat Sh'lomo (Sh'mot), 54–56]

Comment: The reader notes that from the incident of the Burning Bush, Shlomo of Lunst proceeded far beyond the orbit of both its plain meaning and the meanings it acquired in rabbinic commentary. Instead, the narrative is here read as a code for an entire world-view, a radical understanding of existence itself and of a person's understanding him- or herself in the context of that metaphysical teaching conveying that, in an ultimate sense, only God truly exists. Accordingly, the angel in the account is hardly a figure to be grasped literally but is, rather, a person's intuitive understanding of God's ever-presence.

"Fire has many forms. . . . In its lower, external form fire burns, while inner fire, to which this episode alludes, does not burn. And it was this latter fire which appeared to our teacher, Moses, and for this reason Moses was not burnt. This is conveyed in the description, *hamar'eh hagadol haze* ("this great sight") suggesting a higher type of fire. . . .

"The blessed Holy One showed all this to Moses, our Teacher, for the purpose of his people's grasping the power of inner fire, the flaming innerness of fire." [*S'fat emet*, Yehudah Aryeh Lev of Gur (*Sh'mot*), 1874–75]

Comment: In this way, Yehudah Aryeh Lev of Gur, in one of his early homilies, provided a rationale to distinguish between fire that burns and the fire of the Burning Bush which did not burn the plant in which it was situated. More precisely, he explained that the fire within the bush is not the type of fire that burns. It is, instead, a fire that points to a metaphorical use of the word, a non-physical fire that can ignite a human being in other ways. It is the kind of fire within Moses' psyche that ignited his entire being as he displayed in his words and his actions the quality of *hitlahavut* (passion or enthusiasm, related to the word *lahav*, flame).

"Remove your shoes from upon your feet, for the place upon which you stand is a holy place" (Exod 3:5). "Remove your very sense of self. And Moses fulfilled that condition." [*Divrat Sh'lomo* (*Sh'mot*), 57]

"A person must hollow out the materiality of every place, thereby transforming it into a place of holiness." [*No'am Elimelekh* (*Sh'mot*), 119]

Comment: Remove your ego, your very sense of self. In rabbinic texts, the word *makom*, literally "place," came to serve as a word for God, who, the Midrash explains, is everywhere as "there is no place where God is not—not even a thorn-bush" (*Midr. Exod.* 2.5). More implicitly, a recognition of God's omnipresence rules out any ultimate place or reality for self or ego.

A major thrust in Hasidic teaching counters a presumed distinction between what is holy and what is material in nature. It claims that all of existence is potentially holy, and all that is seemingly material has spiritual import and potentiality. A dualistic view of the world contradicts the belief and the experience of God who is the single Source of all being. God's informing Moses that the place of the Burning Bush is holy ground does not establish a particular holiness for that location but, rather, symbolizes the inherent holiness and promise of every location and of every aspect of life.

HUMILITY BEFORE GOD

"And Moses said to God, 'Who am I that I should go to Pharoah and bring the Israelites out of Egypt? . . . (Exod 3:11). "Expressing his own humility, Moses objected that he is not worthy of such a miracle transpiring through him. . . . God granted to him understanding (*binah*) precisely because he so belittled himself." [*Oraḥ l'ḥayyim, Sh'mot*, 103]

" . . . It appears that the holy Torah instructs us how we must behave in God's service. One should approach God in one's prayer and study with love and enthusiasm in one's heart and similarly in all of one's actions which a person does in God's Name. It is proper for that person to question himself as to whether he might have the enthusiasm of strange fire (*eish zarah*)—may it be far from him! And if his heart is continually enthused, he might think it is possible that God brought about this holiness and enthusiasm and that he is included among the holy and righteous ones and fails to consider the possibility that there is something that impugns his behavior. Actually he should be very humble and consider 'how it is possible that a lowly person like me will merit this?'" [*No'am Elimelekh (Sh'mot)*, 121]

Comment: Like other classical Hasidic texts, this passage from *No'am Elimelekh* reveals an awareness of the inner, psychological pitfalls of religious behavior and calling. While in the Torah, Moses is referred to as "the most humble of people" (Num 12:3), Hasidic teaching insists that any and every person drawn to religious behavior and position must question the motivations of his religiosity, as one's deeper motivations might be self-centered and hence unacceptable. It is this need to question and carefully examine oneself that is here read into Moses' own self-questioning of the role given him by God.

OPPRESSION OF THE SOULS

". . . and also I've heard the groan of the Israelites whom Egypt enslaves . . ." (Exod 6:5). "Within the groaning they realize through their understanding and intelligence that also their souls are in Exile." [*Oheiv Yisra'el (Sh'mot)*, 26a]

Comment: While the Torah-text conveys clearly the physical oppression of the Hebrew slaves in Egypt followed by their liberation from that oppression with the Exodus, the Apter *rebbe*, Avraham Yehoshua Heschel of Apt (d. 1825), here pointed specifically to their spiritual oppression, a state-of-being that affects not the body but rather their deeper, total selves. In fact, the emphasis in Hasidic readings on the meaning of servitude and liberation assumes that the decisive oppression is the disastrous effect on one's spiritual self-understanding.

This can be understood partially in that the Hasidic teachers and preachers in Eastern Europe did not at all pretend to be able to bring about changes in the physical, or even legal, relationship of Jews in the places where they lived; they were not revolutionaries devoted to social or political change, but strove instead for a spiritual transformation in the lives of their followers. Their emphasis was directed not to what is outer or external, over which they were essentially powerless, but rather upon their inner lives and consciousness.

THE DEARTH OF JOY

"And (the Israelites) did not listen to Moses due to their impatience and rigorous servitude" (Exod 6:9). ". . . Due to sadness a person fails to accept criticism (and suggestions), and actually this is why his people did not listen to Moses. . . . When one desires to subdue the Shell (*k'lipah*, in this case, an evil shell covering over and eclipsing the omnipresence of the Divine), a person must be joyous, for when that person is joyous, there is no place for sadness and distress. When the one rises, the other falls, and Moses sought to subdue the Shell (represented by Pharoah) by impacting the Israelites with the joy of Redemption. . . .

The Shell itself did not weaken or disintegrate due to the fact that the Israelites failed to make their way to a state of joy . . . ." [*No'am Elimelekh* (*Va'era*), 128]

Comment: Hasidic teaching emphasizes a sense of joy in connection with religious life, a joy exemplified, for example, in the presence of dance in worship, one of the features that the critics of the Hasidic stream deplored. That accent is conveyed, oddly, even when one would reasonably assume that the suffering experienced by the Israelite slaves made such joy impossible. The emphasis on joy and its expressions were likely a very significant factor in the growth of Hasidism, especially but not only among the larger, non-scholarly Jewish population in much of Eastern Europe.

In a later Hasidic homily-text, *Ma'or vashemesh*, containing the homilies of Kalonymus Kalman Epstein of Krakow, the hardships the Israelite slaves encountered were a serious obstacle in the way of experiencing joy even when they made a determined effort to go through the motions of joy. And there, the homilist explained that it was the impassible barrier in the way of true joy that brought God to the realization that it was absolutely necessary to bring the slaves out of Egypt. (*Ma'or va-shemesh*, part II, 1b. A translation and commentary on that text is included in A. Wineman, *Letters of Light*, 68–69.)

THE EXODUS AND RENEWAL IN THE WORLD

"And I have heard the groaning of the Israelites, enslaved by the Egyptians, and I recall My covenant. Therefore say to the Israelites, 'I am the Lord, and I will bring you out from beneath the burdens of Egypt and will relieve you from your bondage and redeem you with an outstretched arm and with great judgements'" (Exod 6:5–6). "Behold it is known that the Exodus from Egypt is the secret of the renewal of the world as a whole as, at that time, it became revealed that God renews His world in accord with the simple Divine Will. He created everything, and all is dependent upon God's Light. . . . It is now recognized that God is gracious and merciful, and in making for a remembrance of God's wondrous acts throughout all the generations it is evident that the very display of the heavens is subject to change through the prayer of a righteous person. . . ." [*Kol simḥah, Vaʾera*, 19ab]

Comment: In the face of an almost universal understanding of the given social order as determined by the stars of the heavens and hence not given to change, Simhah Bunam of Parsishka finds the expression of a remarkable insight in the biblical Exodus-account. That more prevalent attitude and viewpoint, accepted without question, claimed that the state of the world and the order of human society at any given time is the only way things can be, an understanding represented by the belief that the very stars in their order in the sky determine the permanent order of things leaving no space or possibility for change.

Simhah Bunam here defined the Exodus-motif as nothing less than a revolution in human thinking and a clear defiance of such a belief. The fact that bondage was viewed as a fundamental fact about human society does not imply that such has to be and could not be altered or even eliminated. Rather, the homilist went on to suggest a connection between the very possibility of change, even radical change such as the liberation of slaves, with the assertion of the traditional Jewish liturgy that "each day continually God, in His goodness, renews the work of Creation" (*The Authorized Daily Prayer Book*, 108–9). Each dawn is a rebirth of light, a new act of darkness giving way to light. The world is not static and the mode in which a human society is organized is not frozen.

Against that sense of a static world, determined by the particular position of stars in the night-sky, Simhah Bunam attributed to the Exodus-theme the radical role of challenging what was a conventional view and allowing for a basic change both in society and in human consciousness.

GO TO PHARAOH

"Go to Pharoah, for I have hardened his heart and the heart of his servants in order to place My signs (*ototai*) in his midst" **(Exod 10:1).** ". . . that one might attach oneself to the Letters (*oti'ot*), which are vessels containing what is spiritual in nature, as they hold within them the light of the Infinite (*Ein sof*), the life of life itself, and the delight of delights . . . ." [*Tol'dot Ya'akov Yosef (Bo)*, I, 147]

Comment: A play on words and letters reads the signs (*otot*)—in this case the plagues—as letters (*otiot*), more precisely as the letters of the Torah. It furthermore suggests the radical assertion that the core of meaning in the Torah is located not in the words themselves and their surface-meaning, but rather on a deeper level which, Ya'akov Yosef of Polonnoye here suggested, is represented by the letters comprising the words. The words might have a definite, precise meaning, while the letters relate to a deeper, more abstract level not concretized in words. Reflecting its roots in earlier Jewish mystical thought, the Hasidic ethos identified the ultimate truth of the Torah with a level of spiritual experience that fails to confine itself and be defined and concretized in words.

In a somewhat similar vein, Elimelekh of Lyzhansk commented on the words, *Vayityatsvu b'tahtit ha-har* ("And they stood in formation along *the bottom of the mountain*," Exod 19:17) as indicating that God's delight is precisely in the innerness of the Torah (which here parallels the bottom of the mountain). [*No'am Elimelekh, Yitro*, 156]

THE IMPORTANCE OF CULTIVATING A STATE-OF-MIND

"Speak to the Israelites to encamp before *Pi haḥirot* and the sea . . ." (Exod 14:2). "The Torah (in this verse) alludes and teaches us a point of good behavior: when one is about to study Torah or to engage in prayer, one should first prepare the heart with the realization concerning before Whom one is standing. . . . This should occur before a person grants license to one's mouth (to speak) and before one engages in prayer." [*Oheiv Yisra'el (B'shalaḥ)*, 31b]

Comment: In his comment the *Apter rebbe*, Avraham Yehoshua Heschel, referred to the practice of earlier pietists mentioned in the Talmud who, both prior to prayer and after their prayer, contemplated for a whole hour in order to attain and maintain the proper state-of-mind (*b. Ber.*, 32b). He explained the name, *Pi ḥirot*, presumably a place-name in the desert, as a tower, understood metamorphically as prayer, and explained the sea (*ha-yam*) as a reference to *yam ha-talmud* (the Sea of Talmud), the name suggesting that the Talmud, in terms of what it encompasses, is as large and broad as a sea. Both prayer and study hence require a suitable state-of-mind, one characterized by inner piety and are not to be treated lightly either as a matter of rote and habit or as an activity of the mind alone.

THE SONG AT THE SEA

"Then Moses and the Israelites sang this song to the Lord *saying* . . ." (Exod 15:1). "Every place where the word *leimor* (saying) is found in our holy Torah . . . can be explained in that the Torah preceded the world. And if so, how do such tales found in the Torah have any meaning before the world was created? Certainly, though, it is true that the entire Torah consists of names of the blessed Holy One, and the wording of such tales comprises combinations of letters pointing to hidden secrets and mysteries beyond what the human eye can see, but in their descent to this lowly world they were clad in a thick garment as in such tales. Whoever is granted knowledge, understanding and intelligence by God and removes the shield from his eyes will behold wonders in the Torah, even while most of our people grasp the Torah according to its plain meaning. . . . This explains the wording, 'Then Moses sang . . . saying (*leimor*)', explaining that while the Song itself includes hidden mysteries, these were transmitted along the order of *leimor* so that the poorest (spiritually) of the people might also understand (on their own level)." [*K'dushat Levi (B'shalaḥ)*, 115]

Comment: Levi Yitzhak of Berditchev expressed here his view, with roots in kabbalistic thought, that the narrative dimension of the Torah refers to what is quite beyond its literal meaning. As made clear in his remarks, his critique of such literal understanding is rooted not in anything resembling modern biblical criticism, but rather in the metaphysical conception of the Torah as preceding the very existence of the world. Along with that assertion, his statement also assumes that the Torah was written by Moses and dictated by God is a way that even the "common mind," glued and limited to the Torah's literal meaning, might nevertheless be able to understand it on that higher level. The context concerning questions concerning the role of the narratives included in the Torah is discussed more precisely in our concluding chapter.

MANNA

". . . and Moses said to them, 'This is the bread which God gave to you to eat'" (Exod 16:15). "The manna became the source of both physical sustenance and knowledge directing one's behavior on a daily basis, knowledge found in the Torah and drawn from supernal Wisdom." [*Oheiv Yisra'el*, B'shalaḥ, 34b]

Comment: The manna, a flake-like substance which emerged on the ground by early morning, is described as a miraculous type of food at a time when the Israelites, wandering in the desert, were confronting severe hunger, a condition that consequently gave rise to serious complaint. The reader, however, notes in the above comment from *Oheiv*

Yis'rael a discomfort in the mind of Avraham Yehoshua Heschel (d. 1825) with understanding the manna simply as a response to physical hunger, for he added that the same manna, that wondrous food, supplied not only physical nourishment but also an inclination for moral behavior as well. The manna which appeared upon the ground in the morning would have fallen from above and, appropriately, is here described as having its source in a sublime wisdom.

While approaching the subject of manna in terms of a somewhat different direction of thought, a contemporary of the *Apter rebbe*, Kalonymus Kalman of Krakow emphasized that all food, like all material things, has a spiritual element. Though the apparent material character of things tends to conceal their true spiritual element, Holy Sparks are necessarily present within all that is, including all material being, and including even the very food we eat. "The secret of the Divine, of the very life-source (*ḥiyyut*)" is located within food as within everything else," but Kalonymus Kalman viewed manna as a kind of "spiritual bread" (*leḥem ruḥani*) in the sense that with manna one could more readily be aware of that spiritual dimension and hence relate to the very innerness of food and of the act of eating [*Ma'or va-shemesh ('Eikev)*, V, 11b–12a].

The Krakow master's interpretation is not based upon any emphasis upon manna as a miraculous, supernatural happening or phenomenon at a time of severe hunger in the desert, but rather as representing a relationship to eating and to food. The thrust of his discussion implies that all food which we eat is potentially manna, dependent upon the mindset and consciousness which we bring to the act of eating. In every bite we eat we are potentially able to experience the imprint and presence of Divinity.

A somewhat earlier figure, Ze'ev Wolf of Zhitomir (who figures prominently in our concluding chapter) spoke, more emphatically, of the coming down of manna as occurring even now. Far from being connected specifically with a particular span of forty years during which the Israelites journeyed through the wilderness, the manna, to his mind, never ceased. It continues in the form of our livelihood and its skills with which we sustain ourselves in life. Lacking understanding, he explained, a person tends to live with the notion that one subsists and survives in life through that person's own wisdom and ability, "My own power and the might of my own hand have won this wealth for me" (Deut 8:17), not realizing that our very capacities and abilities and the means of our physical survival are a gift of God.

The manna recounted in the Torah is a daily fact in our lives to the extent that we resist perceiving ourselves as "self-made" and self-sustained. To the mind of Ze'ev Wolf, the essence of manna is not a physical but rather a psychological reality, a realization of our own essential dependence [*Or haMe'ir*, *B'shalah*, I, 142]. Rather than a unique and wondrous happening in the distant past, manna is an ever-present daily reality and occurrence in our own lives and represents that awareness of one's dependence upon what is beyond oneself.

Commenting more broadly upon the jar of manna which was to be preserved and placed in front of the Ark in the Tabernacle (Exod 17:33), another Hasidic homilist who died toward the very end of the eighteenth century, Menahem Nahum of Chernobyl, understood that jar to be a vessel that garbs *hiyyut*, the Divine life-energy present within everything in the world. We receive that *hiyyut* daily; else we would not be alive. The Israelites, Menahem Nahum explained, living then in a spiritual rather than a physical state, received that *hiyyut* from its higher Source directly without any garment, whereas today we receive the same *hiyyut* through various garments according to the individual person's capacities and abilities. One's work and means of livelihood comprise, for us, such a vessel garbing the same essential Divine life-energy [*Ma'or 'einayim*, *B'shalah*, 34a].

MOSES AS A JUDGE

"The following day, as Moses proceeded to judge the people, the people stood around him from morning until evening" (Exod 18:13). "As the people, seeking judgment in a dispute, approach and stand in line to be judged by Moses, he would awaken within each person repentance and regret and, consequently, the litigants would arrive at a state of reconciliation on their own." [*Ma'or va-shemesh*, Part II, 17b-18a]

Comment: Kalonymus Kalman Epstein of Krakow depicted the long line of people, all involved in various legal disputes, as they come before Moses, serving here as judge—in fact, as their sole judge. The account in the Torah would suggest that Moses's entire day was given to listening to their claims and counter-claims and arguments and resolving their disputes. Kalonymus Kalman, however, read that scene in a way that involved Moses in a different pursuit: rather than hearing their claims and giving them his verdict, he sought the more difficult task of awakening within the litigants regret and reconciliation, thus making any legal decision unnecessary.

A principal task and function of the traditional *rav* (rabbi) of a community involved his hearing disputes and analyzing each case in terms of rabbinic law. Moses, however, as conceived by Kalonymus Kalman of Krakow, did not fit into that traditional mode and rabbinic legal function. Instead he imagined that Moses sought, in his own way, to speak to the heart of each person and to alter their concerns. No longer, then, did they aspire to win a legal case against their fellow-person but rather they could come to an inner reconciliation that healed the troublesome relationship between the two.

The reader can overhear in Kalonymus Kalman's more difficult but more fruitful approach the preacher's sense of an essential contrast between the leadership of the official religious community and that of the more radical Hasidic stream. While the *rav* wrestled with his mind to arrive at a suitable legal verdict in the face of contrary claims and complaints, the *rebbe* or *tzaddik*, the Hasidic holy man, aspired to touch and change a person's heart.

WHAT TRULY SPEAKS TO A PERSON

"And Jethro heard . . ." (Exod 18:1). "Rashi explained that Jethro/ *Yitro* heard of the parting of the Reed Sea and the war with ʿ*Amalek*. . . . But it appears that a person does not awaken to repentance to bring oneself closer to ways of the worship of God through witnessing miracles and wondrous happenings which occur to others. . . . Rather, the essential element in a spiritual awakening occurs due to the holy man. When such a *tzaddik* lovingly serves

God with awe and inner attachment and truthfully unifies God's great Name, God brings him to true Oneness, awakening further the innerness of the *tzaddik*, and it is this that draws the hearts of people to him—for they, too, are a portion of the Divine." [*No'am Elimelekh* (*Yitro*), 148]

Comment: Jethro is drawn to Moses, we are told, not through the latter's miraculous deeds, but rather through the very essence of the holy man, his inner being. The *tzaddik*, in this passage, is none other than Moses, who now serves as the prototype of the Hasidic holy men. And their followers' attraction to their own *tzaddik* is read into the attraction of Jethro to his daughter's husband, Moses himself, in the biblical account. Jethro, it is understood, was drawn to Moses not due to any of the latter's remarkable achievements as a leader, but rather to something far more inner in character.

MOSES' ASCENT UPON THE MOUNTAIN

". . . and the Lord called Moses to the top of the mountain, and Moses went up" (Exod 19:20). "This has been interpreted according to a talmudic statement that 'the soul of the Messiah occurs in every single generation.' This is not to be understood literally but rather explains that the aspect of the Messiah is present within the collective entity of Israel. And when God decides and wills to redeem his people, he will choose one Israelite worthy of that role and, from above, will reveal His light, the light of the Messiah, upon that person who will then be revealed as such . . . . Correspondingly, in that same sense, Moses was (simply) the one chosen by God at that particular time as the person through whom the Torah would be given." [*Kol Simḥah* (*Yitro*), 22a]

Comment: In contrast with much that was said or implied about Moses, Simhah Bunam here negates the absolute singularity of Moses. Drawing from a similar statement concerning the Messiah in talmudic discussion, the homilist then applied a parallel with the case of Moses. Though the latter ascended on Mt. Sinai to give the Torah to his people, he was not someone uniquely designated from the beginning of time for that role, but simply one who happened to be most worthy in his own time and generation—with the implication that there could easily have been those on his level in other generations and perhaps in all generations.

MOSES IS CALLED TO DESCEND FROM THE MOUNTAIN

"And Moses went up to God, and the Lord called to him from the mountain saying, thus you shall say to the House of Jacob and convey to the Israelites" (Exod 19:3). "Moses, our teacher, seriously prepared himself so that the blessed Holy One might speak with him on an exceedingly high level that no person would grasp, but then God told him not to engage so seriously in his preparation as Moses had wished to do, for if so he would then be unable later to study with the Israelites. Moses had trained himself to speak on God's own level, but that was not God's desire. And so God called to him to descend from the mountain, meaning that he should engage on a lower level which would then enable him to communicate with the Israelites. The words 'the thickness of the cloud' (Exod 19:9) signify a lower level of discourse, so that the Israelites would then understand (in their own way and on their own level) what God revealed to Moses." [*K'dushat Levi* (*Yitro*), 129]

Comment: Moses' initial understanding of his ascent upon the mountain was to relate to God on a level surpassing that of normal human understanding. But that exulted level of understanding is not what was called for in that meeting. The objective was to communicate afterward with Moses' human community with its all-too-human limitations. In the concluding remark on that Torah-portion, *Yitro*, Levi Yitzhak of Berditchev informed his listeners that "even though the Torah truly contains much greater inner connections and combinations (of words, letters and ideas), nevertheless, out of love for Israel, the

Torah was given in a way that the lower worlds might be able to bear it. . . . Some verses later, addressing the people, God says, 'From the heavens I spoke *with you*' (Exod 20:22)—in terms of your own mental grasp . . . ." (*K'dushat Levi* (*Yitro*), 138)

On one hand, the reader grasps that Moses' conception and level of thinking far transcended what he could share with his people, while his task precisely involved communication with his people, with all their limitations. The reader might overhear in this comment a lingering conflict within Levi Yitzhak himself whose thoughts and level of understanding might appear to reach considerably beyond that of his followers' grasp.

"And the Lord said to Moses, 'Behold I will come to you in the thickness of the cloud so that the people will hear as I speak to you . . . . Go to the people and hallow them today and tomorrow . . .'" (Exod 19:10). "When the Divine Word was directed to Moses alone, he could hear it alone in the Tent of Meeting, whereas the Giving of the Torah, by its intrinsic nature, required that the Voice be revealed to the entire multitude of the people. For this reason it was necessary that the Divine Voice descend in the thickness of the cloud so that all the people might hear and, in that way, the entire people would join together with Moses. And precisely due to his joining with all his people, afterward when Moses returned to his own higher level, they, too, would ascend with him in a state of *d'vekut* (a depth-attachment to the Divine)." [*Tol'dot Ya'akov Yosef* (*Yitro*), I, 180, 4th homily]

"The more exalted and unique role of Moses does not isolate him from the large population gathered around the mountain. Moses, as an individual in all his uniqueness, is bound up with an identification with an entire population, as he and that much larger following are bound up one with the other. He must descend because of the multitude, and their sharing in hearing the Word elevates them to a higher level.

"That relationship exemplified a more general relationship which is likened to that of the soul and the body. The body on its own has no vitality or life-quality, without its joining together by an attachment to the soul and, in the wake of that attachment, the soul gives life to the body, something that would not occur were the body to separate from the soul. The body, in this analogy, represents the multitudes of people, whereas the soul represents the (far fewer) individuals of (higher) spiritual quality found in every generation." [Ibid., I, 191, 6th homily]

"This is the intent of a Mishnaic saying in *m Abot* (1:12), 'Hillel said, "Be among the students of Aaron, loving humankind and bringing them near to the Torah"' . . . . At times one must descend to the level of the populace in their multitudes, leaving the (more exclusive) level of a Torah scholar for that of the multitudes. This is necessary to fulfill the command to love those who are of a lower level, more distant from wholeness, but who are nevertheless created by God so that one might bring them nearer to the Torah." [Ibid., I, 197, 6th homily]

". . . this can be understood according to a parable of an official who changed his clothing in order to befriend a prince who had descended to a lesser level and restore the prince to his father. This is the meaning of the words, 'Go to the people and hallow them . . . .' The official did so to be able to elevate those exemplifying a lesser quality of life to the level of holiness, something he could achieve only by his first descending to their level . . . and then he would be able to lift them up and to hallow them, exemplifying what is written, "Go to the people and hallow them." [Ibid., I, 196, 5th homily]

Comment: Without an association with such persons of spiritual quality, Ya'akov Yosef viewed the larger populace as spiritually dead, removed from any channel of real life and understanding. They can be likened to dead bodies, lacking a connection with the soul which bestows life to the body. To the Polonnoye preacher, the more learned figures, whose lives and minds are colored by a greater spiritual depth, have the role of the soul vis-à-vis the population-at-large who are likened to the body. Connecting the points, the emerging Hasidic holy men (*tzaddikim*) correspond to the soul, without which the body itself lacks true life. But at the same time, the role of Moses at Sinai—as singular and unique as that role is—is presented in a way to allude to the interdependence of the Hasidic *tzaddik* and his flock of followers. The master and his followers are both dependent upon one another.

In the homilies from *Tol'dot Ya'akov Yosef* quoted above, Moses' descent from the mountain-top exemplifies the need, when necessary, to descend from one's role as a *ḥaver*, a member of the scholarly class, to the level of the multitude, exemplifying the need to love them in order then to be able to draw them near to the Torah. This theme is suggested in the wording of the verse in the Torah (Exod 19:10), *Lekh el ha'am v'kidsham*, "Go to the people and hallow them." The descent is not an end in itself; the purpose of descent is to enable those on a lower level to ascend to a life of holiness.

It is not difficult to hear in this exegesis a reflection of the evolving conception of the Hasidic holy man, the *tzaddik* or *rebbe*, who is both a leader—or more precisely the center of a community—and at the same time an individual with a depth-relationship with the Divine that transcends the social dimension of his role. Gershom Scholem defined the role of the *tzaddik* as inherently paradoxical in that precisely a person with such a deep inner life serves as the center of a community (Scholem, *Major Trends*, 343). That paradoxical character is read, in turn, into the biblical text relating to Moses, a reading exemplifying a very natural tendency to understand the past and its documents and statements in terms of one's present reality and its needs.

THE GIVING OF THE TORAH (EXOD 19–20)

"The Torah was known already from the time of Abraham, but it was then clad in 'garments of skin' (*kutnot 'or*, Gen 3:21), while the essence of the Receiving of the Torah was the cessation of the skin ('*or* with an '*ayin*) with light (*or*, with an *aleph*), indicating that people now perceived the innerness of the Torah. And so, each year on *Shavu'ot* (the 'Feast of Weeks' traditionally marking the Giving of the Torah), it is necessary to re-acquire the vital innerness of the Torah, for every day one must attain new life and vitality from the holy Torah, recognizing that God brought down to

Israel qualities of heart, light and innerness. That quality of heart was lost with the Making of the Golden Calf which necessitated a broken heart (of regret)." [*Ma'or 'einayim* (*Yitro*), 35a]

Comment: This passage from *Ma'or 'einayim*, the homiletical commentary by Menahem Nahum of Chernobyl, weaves together the theme of *matan torah* (the Giving of the Torah) with the biblical account of the consequences of the primal sin of the First Man (Gen 3:12), together with a later comment indicating that while originally the very first humans were covered with a layer of light (*or*, with the letter *aleph*), their covering later consisted on a layer of skin (*'or*, with the letter *'ayin*). In the above passage from *Ma'or 'einayim*, that change is, in turn, reflected in a change in the way Torah appears in the world. Torah existed prior to Sinai, but in a way that it was covered by "a garment of skin," whereas with the event at Sinai, the innerness itself of the Torah was made evident, allowing for a grasp of the nature of Torah as renewing its inner vitality each and every day.

One easily overhears in this rather unexpected passage a very partisan claim that the earlier manifestation of the Torah suggests the Torah as grasped by the *Mitnagdim*, opponents of the Hasidic stream, while Hasidism, oriented to the quality of innerness, is identified with the Torah as grasped with the Revelation at Sinai. The Giving of the Torah through Moses is, as expected, identical in nature with the Hasidic Torah with its accent upon innerness, while their Opponents' version is thought to bear a relationship precisely with the effects of the Making of the Golden Calf, an episode representing nothing less than utter spiritual betrayal and failure.

The discussion in *Ma'or 'einayim* continues, on the following page (35b of the text), to single out *yir'ah* (reverence and awe) as the internal quality indispensable for grasping the very nature of Torah. Lacking *yir'ah*, the reader is told, it is possible to know all of toraitic and talmudic law even as "one's brain is burnt out in the process" without any essential understanding. Such "Torah," lacking reverence, can be dead, while with true reverence it can be "restored to life."

"At the hour of the Giving of the Torah, the fiftieth gate of Wisdom (the gate to that which is beyond human grasp and which, until then, was closed even to Moses) was opened to him, for he had already perfected his grasp of all the available forty-nine gates of Understanding. That fiftieth gate was now fully available to him both in generality and in detail. That same gate was then available also to the other Israelites, although to a reduced degree, in accordance with each person's own level, even though they all had entered into the world of (inner) freedom. The fiftieth gate, that of supreme wisdom, *Sha'ar haAyin* ('the Gate of Nothingness'), was then open to each person through a thick screen of holy reverence, the degree of thickness varying in proportion to the level of that person's preparation and (spiritual) grasp." [*Ḥesed l'Avraham*, Introduction, 13]

Comment: While, according to tradition, forty-nine Gates of Wisdom were open to Moses, here Avraham ha-Malakh, the son of Dov Baer of Mezhirech, provided for Moses and, to a more qualified extent also to the Israelites, also that fiftieth Gate, a level of Wisdom which is normally beyond the reach of human grasp, the apex of humility transcending all sense of self.

EVERY SEVENTH DAY

"And you shall speak to the Israelites saying, you shall observe My Sabbath, for it is a sign between Me and you for all your generations to know (*lada'at*) that I am the Lord who hallows you" (Exod 31:13). "Each *Shabbat* (Seventh Day) the aspect of Moses is revealed, restoring to Israel two crowns, the crown of love and that of awe. That aspect comes in the form of the Additional Soul (*n'shamah y'teirah*) experienced by every member of Israel who then acquires *da'at* (spiritual understanding) .... And each *Shabbat*, the aspect and experience of standing at Sinai (*ma'amad Har Sinai*) recurs. For then, they accepted God's divinity, liberating them from evil, and now, with *Shabbat*, they similarly experience freedom from the Evil Force (*Sitra aḥ'ra*)." [*Ma'or 'einayim* (*Ki Tissa*), 39b]

Comment: The liberation which Moses brought to his people is understood here as a freedom from the Evil Impulse which can easily make its presence in life and in the affairs of the world. Menahem Nahum of Chernobyl, in this passage, read that liberation not as a one-time happening but rather as recurrent, against the background of evil which is similarly recurrent. While the verse in the Torah mentions the infinitive, *lada'at* (to know), that term came to indicate spiritual understanding (*da'at*). The Exodus itself, presented as much more than the departure from a place and situation of physical bondage, is grasped as a radical departure from spiritual bondage. At any point-in-time we can find ourselves enslaved to the evil within ourselves, while the weekly observance of the Seventh Day becomes a recurrent experience of liberation and of spiritual insight represented by Sinai.

RULES CONCERNING THE BUILDING OF ALTARS

"And if you make for Me an altar of stones, do not build it of stones that have been hewn, as by employing your sword over them you will have profaned the altar" (Exod 20:25). "The interpretation: your learning should not be used to display your *pilpul* (casuistic, argumentative ability) for if so, it has become like hewn stones.

". . . as by employing your sword over them . . . ." "The interpretation: employing your exaggerated sharpness of mind and argument for purposes of your own pride and arrogance,

"you will have profaned the altar"—"then you will have profaned the Torah, God forbid!" [*No'am Elimelekh* (*Yitro*), 158]

Comment: This verse, one of a few brief laws directly following the Decalogue is here read symbolically by Elimelekh of Lyzhansk in the light of the very bitter polemic between the followers of Hasidism, in its fairly early period, and their opponents (*"Mitnagdim"*) who viewed Hasidism as heretical and lacking in all virtue and knowledge. They suggested that the Ḥasidim (pietists) felt only scorn for the more learned ones of the traditional camp and for their learning which Elimelekh viewed as often characterized by intricate and sometimes never-ending logical argumentation (*pilpul*) of endless complexity to the exclusion of more spiritual and emotional emphases.

Such study, in the eyes of the Ḥasidim, was easily expressive of ego and pride and was thought of as consisting of argumentation for its own sake and is, furthermore, warlike as its participants engaged in constant mental battle with one another. Hence, such argumentative study is here likened to cutting stones with a sword. In his brief explanation, Elimelekh was characterizing his perception of the intellectual life of the opposing traditional camp as a profanation of the Torah itself.

In *Tiferet Uzi'el* (*Yitro*, 17a) Uziel ben Zvi connected the prohibition of building an altar of hewn stones with another prohibition that follows immediately, that of revealing one's nakedness in ascending the steps to an altar (Exod 20:26). Uziel understood the requirement that an altar be made of earth rather than of stone as a sign to impress upon the person that he himself is likened to earth, "and when it enters your mind that you are a person of rank, a learned person, a scribe and person of wisdom, you may not ascend but should rather lower yourself as though you were actually earthen matter."

Furthermore, relating this explanation to the prohibition that follows, you should not engage in study thinking of your own importance and rank, for in doing so, you are, in effect, revealing your (spiritual) nakedness. "One should rather see himself as lowly and as delinquent in his worship of the One who truly and uniquely occupies a high level and who bestows blessings upon us."

An earthen altar—the reader easily understands—reflects the image of Moses, said to be the very humblest of all persons (Num 12:3), and ascending the steps to the altar with pride serves as the very counter-image to Moses.

THE MAKING OF THE GOLDEN-CALF

"Do not be angry; you know that the people has an evil character (Exod 32:22). . . . Indeed this people perpetrated a grave sin

and made for themselves a god of gold" (Exod 32:31). "Aaron the priest was a person of kindness and a prophet of God. And even if a person occasionally commits a sin, it is not proper to accuse him to such a degree, for he was brought to that act through the fact that his material being has not been separated and purified from the evil aspects found within himself. And, to my mind, Aaron's intent, in ascribing to the people an evil character, was to acknowledge that they still have to contend with their own inner aspects, and for this reason they came to failure with this sin. But, at the same time, considering the good within themselves they should not have brought themselves to that deed. Would that God enable them to free themselves completely from their evil aspect and cleave, instead, from now on, to the true and lasting good. May this be God's will . . . .

"Seemingly, it is surprising that Moses our Teacher, the faithful shepherd, would level such serious criticism of Israel after, on several occasions, he devoted his very being for them. It is even stranger that he then came to seek God's forgiveness on their behalf. He could have minimized their sin as far as possible in order to strengthen his request of forgiveness for the seed of Israel.

"Indeed, when a person comes to understand and reflect in his heart, he will know and understand that, in truth, for one who has transgressed there is no more difficult punishment than the transgression itself, when his mind fully realizes what he has done. . . . It follows that one who has severed and distanced himself from the Root of Life and has fallen within the Shells and forces of externality will certainly be clad in great shame and regret . . . .

"And this sense of shame is, indeed, the most severe punishment, as our Sages said, 'the reward of transgression (*'aveirah*) is transgression (itself)" [*m. Abot* 4:2]. "For in his eyes, the whole world itself becomes smaller than the extent of the heart's pain . . . ." [*Oheiv Yisra'el (Ki Tissa)*, 56a]

Comment: The toraitic narrative, as found in Exod 32, views the Making of the Golden Calf (*ma'aseh ha'egal*) as an act of utter spiritual disloyalty and treason. When Moses did not immediately descend from

Mount Sinai, the Hebrews turned to fashion for themselves what could easily be understood as a pagan god of gold as an object of their worship. And Aaron, at least on the surface of the narrative, succumbed to the demand of the Israelite mob to make for them such a god of gold. That action, in turn, invites a Divine determination to abandon the population of former slaves leaving them to perish in the wilderness. Only Moses' pleading, offering his own death and rejecting God's offering to make of him and his own posterity a great people in place of the Israelites, turns God away from His angry determination.

In later Jewish thought and interpretation, the Making of the Golden Calf was thought to have brought on a complete setback in the very nature of existence, a de-spiritualization of being itself, leaving us with much more limited understanding. This concept received a central place in the thought of Yitzhak of Radvil (*Or Yitzhak*) who maintained that the sin of *ma'aseh ha'egal* altered our understanding of the Torah in a fundamental way. (And note also an earlier source, *Shn'e luhot ha-brit*, II, 337a.)

In view of that harsh condemnation, in the above passage from *Ohev Yisra'el*, Avraham Yehoshua Heschel of Apt (d. 1825) seems here to have offered a much more moderate and apologetic understanding and response to what others considered to be that gravest of sins. In his comments on that episode, he envisioned Aaron as emphasizing the need to consider the larger human condition as typified by perpetual conflict between the spiritual and physical elements of the human makeup which makes for an ongoing and never-ending struggle within the self.

The preacher, moreover, interprets Moses' role as pointing to a psychological realization that the truer and deeper punishment is what occurs within the person who had surrendered to sin, the shame that forever remains with him and torments his heart. Moses stresses the point that no external punishment cast upon the Israelites for their act of disloyalty could measure up to the real yoke of punishment which they will inevitably bear, namely that internal sense of self-shame that will forever be a part of their very being.

MOSES' RADIANT COUNTENANCE

"Upon descending, Moses did not know that the light of his countenance became radiant as he spoke (with God)," (Exod 34:29). "They then knew concerning Moses that also even at his birth he had the qualities of goodness and truth, though they were hidden and concealed and only now were revealed." [*Degel maḥaneh Efrayim (Ki Tissa)*, 137]

"Even though Moses, our teacher, never sinned, nevertheless, as the head of all Israel, all the souls of Israel were included in him together with their sins and their merits, and they depended upon him when he spoke, seeking (forgiveness) for all Israel." [*Divrat Sh'lomo (Ki Tissa)*, 105]

"When the *tzaddik* (holy man) is speaking with humans words of holiness and awe of the Eternal One, he comes to feel a pronounced enthusiasm. The flaming enthusiasm in Moses' heart brought on in its wake the illumination of his face, though Moses himself was not aware of this." [*No'am Elimelekh (Ki Tissa)*, 192]

Comment: While other explanations tend to explain the radiance of Moses' face after coming down from the mountain as an effect of his having been standing alone in the presence of God, this comment of Elimelekh of Lyzhansk offers an explanation on quite a different plane. It is removed from a sense of absolute uniqueness as the effect of Moses' having stood in God's presence in a very singular way. Rather, in keeping with the ethos of Hasidism, it was due to a detail of Moses' own doing, his own kindling, within himself, an inner enthusiasm (*hitlahavut*, from *lahav*, flame). It is, consequently, a condition ultimately open, to one degree or another, to any and every person.

MOSES' REQUEST OF GOD IS REFUSED

"And I pleaded with the Lord at that time, saying, . . . 'Let me cross over and see the good land beyond the Jordan, this good mountain and the Lebanon.' And the Lord, angry with me because of you, would not listen to me, saying, 'you've said enough;

do not speak to me any more on this matter'" (Deut 3:23, 25–26). "While his prayer (of request) was unanswered, it elevated and repaired all the prayers of the Israelites to be able to enter the Land. For Moses devoted his life to the Israelites, and even his very request itself was for their benefit. He knew that without him they would damage their way, and therefore his prayer aided them, and even though his (particular) request was not answered, it was not without benefit." [S'fat emet, V, Va'ethanan, 1873–74, abridged]

Comment: In his collection of homilies, dating from the latter decades of the nineteenth century up to the master's death in 1905, Yehudah Aryeh Lev of Gur was emphatic in his understanding Moses' request to enter the Land together with his people as related not to his own personal benefit or desire, but rather as spoken solely out of consideration for his people. Only in those terms could the preacher and commentator understand Moses' request, made by a supremely holy person.

In a homily on the same Torah-portion which he gave two years later (1878–79), the same preacher suggested that God was displeased in Moses' lowering himself by pleading as he did. Moses could have made a case on the basis of his own worthy actions rather than as what sounded like a request of a favor of which neither he nor his people were deserving. The homilist suggested that Moses knew that were he to enter the Land with his followers, he would repair his people and, consequently, there would be no further exile.

The contrasting tenor of that homily, which viewed Moses' request as thoroughly valid in terms of his actions and accomplishments over the years, might appear to question the value and legitimacy of Moses' humility. However, it interprets Moses' request, humbly made, as expressing a realization on his part that ultimately it is not man's deeds but God's Will that is the determining factor.

MOSES APPROACHING THE END OF HIS LIFE

"And Moses went (*vayeilakh*) and he spoke all these words to all Israel. And he said to them, 'I am one-hundred-twenty years old this day and I will no longer be able to come and go, and the Lord said to me, "you shall not cross this (River) Jordan" (Deut 31:1–2). . . . And the Lord said to Moses, 'behold your days are approaching death . . .'" (Deut 31:14). "And Moses went (to his death) as a person who goes from one room to another, as he did not taste death at all. . . . And Moses went, meaning that he *went* with his entire soul and he was no longer connected to this world at all. . . . He walked (died) with a total attachment to the Creator." [*Divrat Sh'lomo* (*Vayeilakh*), 108–9]

Comment: Shlomo of Luntz went on to explain that Moses experienced and exemplified the summit of love as he connected with God with all his strength and his life-energy (*ḥiyyut*) and, furthermore, that the words he said on that last day of his life encompassed all the pronouncements that he had made during all the years of his life. His life-span of one-hundred-twenty years became as one; that single day encompassed his entire life in which he totally cleaved to the *Shekhinah* (the Divine Presence).

We then hear that for Moses, the difference between his existence in this world and in what followed was no more than that of one's walking from one room to another. While in several places, the Torah perhaps very unconvincingly explains his death before being able to enter into the Land with his people as punishment for certain shortcomings in his actions, Shlomo of Luntz painted a picture of Moses as one who attained the very pinnacle of holiness throughout his life to the extent that he was already completely attached to the Divine. To that preacher's mind, a complete and unblemished attachment to God, something inherently associated with one's situation in a more ultimate state-of-being, was expressed in Moses' quality of compassion which had colored his entire life.

The view of Moses expressed in this way might echo and share, to a degree, some three passages in rabbinic texts (*Sifre D'varim*, #357, *Midrash Tanna'im*, 224, and *b. Sotah*, 13b; note Ginzberg, *Legends*, VI,

161–162, n. 951) which mentions an opinion that "Moses, our teacher, never died, but he stands and serves above." The account in *Divrat Sh'lomo* does not negate Moses' death as such, but rather claims that his death did not make for any significant change in his status and his being. For Moses, death was no more than "walking from one room to another."

And it is interesting to note that *Shivhei haBesht* (an account of the life of the Ba'al Shem Tov, considered the father of Hasidism, which appeared in print in 1814–15) relates that a large clock suddenly stopped just before the very last breaths of the Ba'al Shem Tov. When his followers positioned themselves around the clock to prevent his noticing that it stopped, he told them, "I know that I will be leaving this entrance and will immediately go into another entrance" [*Sefer shivhei haBesht*, ed. Horodezky, 168; *In Praise of the Ba'al Shem Tov*, 257]. Did the later followers of the *Besht* posit a similarity between their description of the death of their founder and that of Moses?

MOSES' TRANSCENDS HIS SENSE OF SELF

"There has never risen another prophet like Moses whom the Lord knew face-to-face" (Deut 34:10). "Moses was unique in the qualities both of humility and reverence, and in the wake of those qualities his grasp and prophecy were of a higher rank than that of all the other Prophets. At the time of the Giving of the Torah he saw himself in the company of God's presence, as though he himself did not even exist. And had he attained any greater degree of humility, he would (literally) have ceased to exist.

"But he could not completely attain the height of reverence, for the deeds and qualities of the Israelites had not been perfected, and had he reached that still higher level, they would have been unable to accept and bear his rule and guidance. For this reason he had to attain a state lacking the ideal level of humility until he was truly the head of the people (Deut 33:21)." [*Hesed l'Avraham*, Introduction, 14]

"Just as no grain can grow except by its losing its form and shape and arriving at a state of non-being, so there can be no

Revelation in this world except through the *tzaddik* (righteous person) who has attained that level of non-being." [Ibid. (*Va'era*), 55]

Comment: Moses' absolute uniqueness—to the mind of Avraham ha-Malakh—is here intimately bound up with his humility, and that quality of humility at its fullest—the absolute absence of any sense of self—is, in turn, understood psychologically as a virtual negation of one's very existence. That sense of non-being, in its Hasidic treatment, is further associated with Revelation. As a result, the tradition of Moses' connection with the Giving of the Torah becomes associated with the Prophet's overcoming his own very self-awareness, as the Prophet has grown to a space where he experiences another type of awareness which transcends all sense of self.

WHY DID MOSES DIE?

". . . and no one knows his burial-site until this day" (Deut 34:6). "There is a view that there is no death without sin (*ein mavet b'li ḥet*), and every person dies due to some sin which that person committed. Another view suggests that humans must die, for in life, due to the materiality of the body, they cannot attain the secrets of the Torah, secrets which they can acquire only following death, as death allows for a more complete attachment to God.

"Neither of these views explains Moses' death. (If he was not allowed to come to the Land as a consequence of his striking a rock to produce water from it [Num 20:10–13], why must he also die as well?) Of Moses it is written, '. . . in all My house, he is (the most) faithful' (Num 12:3). And Moses, who in his lifetime 'spoke face-to-face with God,' attained all the secrets of the Torah, even those derived through a brilliant student long after his time.

"The words, 'No person knows the location of his burial' (Deut 34:6) can be understood to mean that no person knows why Moses died." [*Tiferet Uziel* (*Zot haB'rakhah*), 42b]

While avoiding certain rather surprising examples of commentary and re-telling of the biblical narrative which will be brought out later in this journey, this collection of examples of Hasidic interpretation indicate the degree that virtually everything found in the account of Moses in the biblical narrative came to be understood by the Hasidic homilists as comprising a statement reflecting, in some way, their own particular complex of values and their own self-image. Whether consciously or subconsciously, they read themselves and their stream and set of values into the canonized text and its account of Moses.

4

The "World of History" and the Hasidic Homily

Egyptian Bondage and the Exodus[1]

Gershom Scholem, who pioneered the modern study of Jewish mystic traditions, pointed to an essential indifference and even contempt on the part of mystics to "the world of history."[2]

On a literary level, what Scholem called "the world of history" bears a special relationship to narrative. While narrative as such is not necessarily historical, a sense of "the world of history" necessarily locates happenings of sacred import within a temporal order. Narrative relates a series of inter-connected happenings, whether historical or imaginary, having a temporal sequence, as the account revolves around a happening or series of happenings situated at a particular, though not necessarily closely-defined point in time.

In contrast, the Hasidic homilists essentially read the same scriptural narratives, set at a particular central point-in-time, as

---

1. An earlier version of this chapter, "The Exodus in the Lens of Hasidic Teaching," appeared in *Conservative Judaism* 52.3 (2000) 39–45.

2. Scholem, *Major Trends*, 19.

symbolic statements conveying what is actually recurrent and perpetually present, occurring even in the inner life of each person.

These homilists, with their roots in Jewish mystic thought, did not turn their focus away from biblical narrative out of any critical assessments. Their rejection, as it were, of the "world of history" in their approach to the biblical text rested on quite different considerations. Dov Baer, the Maggid of Mezhirech, who so significantly left his stamp upon classical Hasidic thought, made the following comment concerning the narratives in the Torah:

> The Torah is primordial, and it is not within time, and so how does a story have a place in what is prior to time itself? It must be the case, rather, that this story is perpetually present—and, furthermore, that the same story is present within the human being, who is called a microcosm.[3]

To the mind of the Maggid, a narrative episode found in the text of the Torah must necessarily have a deeper meaning, and the passage as understood merely on the level of the *p'shat*, the literal surface-meaning, would in itself be quite irrelevant. The Maggid made the above comment in connection with an episode in the life of the biblical Jacob, but we might inquire also concerning toraitic narratives that focus not on the lives of individual persons, but on the Israelites as a people, for example the Torah's account of the servitude of the Israelites of ancient Egypt. That kind of account reaches beyond the category of "tales" to a more obvious sacred history, but Hasidic homilies grasp that even such a narrative of the collective is not to be read simply on its surface-level but that its more essential significance lies elsewhere.

READING HISTORICAL NARRATIVE IN TERMS OF INNER MEANING

The scenario of Egyptian bondage and the Exodus and that of the Revelation at Sinai are cornerstones of the Israelite experience and

---

3. *Or torah* (*Vayetze*), 9a.

of Jewish sacred history. Both *y'tzi'at Mitzrayim,* the account of slavery and redemption (as found in Exod 1–16) and *ma'amad har Sinai,* the biblical account of the Revelation-scene at Sinai (found in Exod 19, 20, and 24, and Deut 5) are clearly narrative in character. And furthermore, these two accounts as found both in the Torah and in later Jewish lore and tradition comprise together what can be regarded as *the* foundational story both of biblical Israelite religion and of historical Judaism.

Among the tendencies evident, even though not explicitly defined, in the classical Hasidic treatments of these two biblical accounts are those that, exemplifying Scholem's statement, suggest themselves as conscious or unconscious literary strategies in reading a narrative passage relating to "the world of history" in ways that often substantially negate the very character of history and of narrative itself. Some of these tendencies build upon traits and strands present in earlier Jewish interpretation of biblical text, but beyond those, some essential qualities of the Hasidic homily and its orientation intrinsically run counter to narrative and to what Scholem called "the world of history."

If we define as "history" for our purposes not necessarily verified or verifiable records of happenings but rather the potential stuff of history, what can be situated in time, then we can discover in the Hasidic homilies on Israelite servitude in Egypt various relationships to the "history" found in the Torah. The most prevalent of these would be the homily's attempt to define a deeper, inner meaning of the account. While the historical dimension is generally assumed, the Hasidic homily also presumes that it is the inner, deeper meaning of such an historical account that is of prime significance. Qualitatively the history-like account in the Torah could be likened to that part of an iceberg visible above the water's surface, while the inner, deeper meaning of the same text resembles the much vaster part of the iceberg, hidden in the depths of the water.

EXAMPLES FROM HASIDIC HOMILY-TEXTS

Yitzhak of Radvil, for example, among others identified the true distress of the Israelites in Egypt as their awareness that the *Shekhinah* (the Divine Presence and Immanence) was also in exile. Drawing upon an earlier kabbalistic concept, a greater, Divine Exile is at the very heart of the human experience of exile.[4] In this general vein, Efrayim of Sedilikov identified the real nature of the exile in Egypt with all its tribulations as the lack of *Da'at*, of knowledge of God—or more precisely, the absence of an inner awareness that ultimately there is nothing at all apart from God's Presence. And he defined the deeper meaning of the Exodus from Egypt precisely as the disclosure, and hence liberation, of *Da'at*.[5] Menahem Nahum of Chernobyl suggested that with the liberation of *Da'at*, the Israelites were then able to receive the Torah which was translated, through the very quality of *Da'at* itself, into a form that the Israelites could understand in terms of (the limitations of) their physical, human experience.[6]

A commonplace found in the homilies of the Hasidic masters relates the Hebrew name for Egypt, *Mitzrayim*, to the word *meitsarei yam* (narrow straits of the sea), as the biblical account is largely grasped in terms relating to spiritual narrowness, not to a geographical location but rather to a state of mind and culture lacking spiritual awareness.

At other times, the homilist's concerns focus upon what is perceived to be a parallel to the historical happening that is recounted on the level of *p'shat*. A key statement included in the writings of Ya'akov Yosef of Polonnoye and attributed to the Ba'al Shem Tov speaks of two kinds of redemption, that of the collective entity, the Israelite nation, and the spiritual redemption of the individual person. There are, likewise, two kinds of exile: one affects a total population, while the second is a personal exile in which one's soul is in a state of internal enslavement at the hands of the

---

4. *Or Yitzḥak (Sh'mot)*, 95–96.

5. *Degel maḥaneh Efrayim (Bo)*, 92.

6. *Ma'or 'einayim (Sh'mot)*, 28a

person's evil inclination and stands in need of redemption from that captivity."[7] And on another plane, the Maggid of Mezhirech grasped such episodes as the scenario of Egyptian bondage and the Exodus as "perpetually present."

Most frequently the homilies' concern is with spiritual enslavement and redemption, in effect reading the account of collective physical servitude as a parable or prototype of a deeper and more general spiritual condition. *Mitzrayim*, in this sense, often signifies the material world and the level of existence to which the soul, rooted in the Divine, can easily become subjected. Efrayim of Sedilikov read the Torah's mention of Egyptian bondage as a person's subjection to the four elements compromising his physical being and to the physical desires and evil propensities which they engender. And the same preacher grasped *Mitzrayim* metaphorically as the condition of a person's life and consciousness being thoroughly bound up with and limited to the needs of that person's natural, physical state. The Exodus, in turn, suggests transcending that more limited horizon of concern and one's becoming oriented to a higher meaning and service directed toward God and connected with a person's deeper self.[8]

The biblical account of exile in ancient Egypt has also suggested the descent and exile of the soul to this material world, a descent that is necessary for the reason that only from within the physical reality of this lower world can the soul truly fulfill its holy task,[9] that of infusing this material realm with the spiritual quality of the higher worlds.[10] By extension, the teachers of early Hasidism read in the descent of the Israelites to Egypt an allusion to the spiritually elevated soul's making contact with the Jewish multitudes situated on a lower level in order to be able to influence and elevate them, a paradigm of Hasidism's conception of the role of its own type of leadership.[11]

7. *Tol'dot Ya'akov Yosef* (Sh'mini), I, 296.

8. *Degel Maḥaneh Efrayim* (Sh'mot), 83.

9. *Tol'dot Ya'akov Yosef* (Sh'mot), I, 133, 135, 136.

10. *Ma'or 'einayim* (Sh'mot), 28a.

11. *Tol'dot Ya'akov Yosef* (Sh'mot), I, 139.

Making for a further distancing from the *p'shat* in the Hasidic homily, the suggested inner meaning of the text might or might not even be in consonance with the tenor of the text's surface level. For example: some interpretations read servitude (*'avdut*, from the same root as *'avodah* suggesting a much wider range of meaning) in Egypt in a way to suggest something of an emphatically positive nature, and went so far as viewing the Israelites' descent to Egypt as an act of *tikkun*, of mending and rectifying the basic condition of existence. Menahem Nahum of Chernobyl, for example, interpreted the Israelites' experience in Egypt as a *tikkun* (repair) of the effects of the primordial Shattering (*sh'virah*) of the Vessels which, in Lurianic Kabbalah, had cast the "Letters of Torah," an intrinsic aspect of all being, into exile.[12] According to Yitzhak of Radvil, that *tikkun* consisted of a unification of seemingly diverse aspects of the Godhead, of uniting body and soul, the earthly with the heavenly, the lower with the higher worlds to restore that primordial unity which was marred when all things became severed from their true, Divine Root.[13]

The Hebrew noun *'avodah* can refer to slavery or indentured servitude, to work itself or to worship, both in the more limited cultic sense and also in the most all-encompassing sense. And allowing the wording of the text, and sometimes allowing even a single word and its connotations to take priority over the tenor of the plain sense of the text and its context, *'avdut* (normally thought of as "servitude, slavery") is, at times, actually read as referring to the very summit of freedom! The Israelites, in their Egyptian experience, both engaged in *tikkun* (repair) and fulfilled the meaning of *'avodah* as worshipful service to God, acting in effect as a model for future generations of the family of Israel.

A homilist from a later period, Yitzhak Ya'akov of Biala, explained the verse, "And (the Egyptians) embittered their lives with difficult work, with mortar (*homer*) and bricks (*l'veinim*) . . ." (Exod 1:14), as referring to "the capacity of Israel to transform matter (*homer*) into form and to make it iridescent, polished and purified

12. *Ma'or 'einayim* (*Sh'mot*), 28b.

13. *Or Yitzhak* (*Sh'mot*), 92–93.

(*m'luban*) . . . ."[14] This brief comment, utilizing a correspondence of homonyms, reads into a biblical statement of the torturous labor assigned by the Egyptians an exalted Divine task given to the Jew of all eras, that of providing form and order to our material existence and physicality so that matter itself might acquire a soul-like quality.

In another insightful example of Hasidic interpretation, Simhah Bunam of Parsishka, an important figure in the annals of early Polish Hasidism, defined the rejoicing at the Sea of Reeds as celebrating precisely a shift of consciousness in the minds of the Israelites as they left behind a sense of their own unworthiness, their despair and their stifling fear of the Egyptians. The latter, now, "were as nothing in their eyes. *And that itself was the great salvation* (occurring) *in the heart!*" They now saw the Egyptian oppressors "*as though* they had died" and thought of them as corpses.[15] Simhah Bunam appears to have suggested that the real and decisive action in the account of the splitting of the waters of the Sea of Reeds (*yam-suf*) occurred, in effect, within the consciousness of the Israelites!

Though the Hasidic masters did not confront issues of biblical and historical criticism, they nevertheless understood the significance of the biblical account of bondage and deliverance in ways that far transcend the literal sense of the text as basically a statement of physical happenings relating to a single point in time.

DEEPER EXPRESSIONS OF THE CONTRAST

A later Hasidic master, Yehudah Aryeh Leib Alter of Gur (d. 1905),[16] the third *rebbe* or leader of the *Gerer Ḥasidim*, developed a more systematic interpretation of exile and deliverance. He taught that one who connects with the innerness of experience, with the ever-present Divine life-source (*ḥiyyut*), can experience perpetual

---

14. *Divre binah* on Exod 1:14 (*Sh'mot*), quoted in *P'nine haHasidut*, II, 8.

15. *Kol simḥah* (*B'shalaḥ*), 67.

16. *S'fat emet*, first edition, 1905–8. Homilies listed by year.

renewal, and such renewal negates the very nature of exile as he understood it.[17]

What is particularly striking about the homilies of Yehudah Aryeh Leib Alter on Exod 1–16, is the way these homilies repeatedly celebrate aspects of redemption that are present even within exile and distress. In any number of comments, this Hasidic master emphasized the inner, spiritual strength of the Israelites even in their dreadful situation—a source of inner strength which, he would accentuate, is a resource available for those experiencing external distress.[18] "Within the very souls of the Israelites was a soul-strength that awakened the person to make an opening, even so small as the point of a needle, allowing the soul to radiate within the person."[19] And Yehudah Aryeh Lev told his followers that the Israelites "were sent to *Mitzrayim* so that, like the stars which are iridescent in the darkness, they too might discover the (Divine) iridescence even there"—even within the darkness.[20]

Even within exile and bondage, a person must seek an inner space for one's own soulfulness, an inner space over which oppressors can have no control. For Yehudah Aryeh Lev, both *Shabbat* (the Seventh Day) and Torah-study, along with the theme of the Exodus, embody that life of inner freedom, as they can lift a person above the limitations of one's present, external reality.[21]

If the earlier Hasidic masters placed significance upon what they viewed as the inner meaning of the toraitic text recounting exile and redemption, Yehudah Aryeh Lev went further as he associated exile itself with an *external* orientation to experience, just as he identified redemption as being attuned, instead, to that innerness of all experience which he identified with God's immanence.[22]

The same Hasidic master who crafted a theology of history also lifted up the basic themes of exile, oppression, and deliverance

17. Ibid., *Sh'mot,* 1871.

18. Ibid., 1871.

19. Ibid., 1904.

20. Ibid., 1872.

21. Ibid., 1874, 1881, 1904.

22. Ibid., 1871.

from their context in what is time-bound in character, lifting them beyond any particular point of time. "We are commanded to remember, each day, the Exodus from *Mitzrayim*, precisely because the Exodus actually occurs each day as the blessed Holy One daily redeems each individual according to that person's serving God with pure motivation."[23] And conversely, "each and every day includes some form of concealment of the Divine through the sense of the ordinariness of time and requires Redemption."[24]

Each day we experience bondage unless we succeed in transcending that ordinariness of time, the sense of sameness and regularity and externality (which mark the world when thought of as severed from the Divine), just as the experience of renewal which typified the Exodus from Egypt is a possibility each and every day.[25] The same preacher and commentator interpreted bondage as subjugation of the soul by the body, and he claimed that whenever people assign priority to the physical rather than to what belongs to a deeper level of the self, they are slaves, even if they enjoy the privileges of freedom.[26]

Such statements in his homilies suggest the possibility both of experiencing aspects of Redemption even within external bondage and exile, and of experiencing aspects of subjugation even within external freedom. Objectivity cannot totally prevail over subjectivity. "The Redemption from *Mitzrayim* is the experience of a holy illumination within the very straits (*meitzarim*) and within the state of hiddenness of the Divine."[27] One's external or objective reality needn't have complete control over a person's inner life and mindset, and it is precisely in a person's innerness that he or she is truly slave or free.

The contemporary reader might find in the homilies of Yehudah Aryeh Lev, collected in *S'fat smet*, an affinity with themes found in certain streams of more contemporary psychological thought,

23. Ibid., 1885.

24. Ibid., *Bo*, 1895.

25. Ibid., 1898.

26. Ibid., *Sh'mot*, 1904.

27. Ibid., *Bo*, 1872.

ideas found in the writings of Thomas Moore, who so accentuates nurturing and protecting one's soulfulness,[28] and of Viktor Frankl, the Viennese psychiatrist who was himself a concentration-camp inmate and who, from his observation of his fellow-prisoners, so emphasized the crucial role of a sense of meaning in life in enabling a person to cope even with the most limiting and even brutal and tormenting external conditions.[29]

The reader of Hasidic homilies on those chapters from the Torah that recount the saga of Egyptian bondage and the Exodus is struck by an overriding concern not with history as such, but rather with the inner life. Together with the tradition of earlier kabbalistic interpretation that it inherited, the Hasidic homily represents a paradigm-shift away from history, which relates to one-time happenings. And, in its place, it sought to overhear in the Torah-text an insight into the nature of the human condition which is true of all time.

The Exodus from Egypt has been described by the *Apter rebbe*, Avraham Yehoshu'a Heschel (d. 1825), as one dimension of a movement that occurs on various levels in a way appropriate to that level. At its all-encompassing cosmic plane, it signifies the liberation of the soul-sparks from their imprisonment in the Shells (*k'lipot*) of darkness which occurred with the initial moves of the Infinite Godhead to bring a world into existence. It occurs, in addition, when a person outgrows his childish, largely ego-centered view of reality (*mohin d'kaknut*), replacing it with a more responsible understanding of life, one centered not around oneself and one's own desires but rather around the higher Will of the Divine.

In this way the Exodus, on one level or another, occurs continually.[30]

---

28. I. Moore, *Care of the Soul.*

29. V. Frankl, *Man's Search for Meaning.*

30. *Oheiv Yisra'el* (*Vayetze*), 15a; also (*Bo*), 29b.

5

The "World of History" and the Hasidic Homily

The Revelation-Scene at Sinai[1]

A NARRATIVE RECAST TO REFER TO ALL OF TIME

Reading the account of the Revelation-scene at Sinai (*ma'amad har Sinai*) as found principally in Exodus, ch. 19, one takes note of various elements such as the desert, the mountain, the fire burning upon the mountain, along with smoke and the loud shofar-sound—all details pertaining to the setting of the Sinaitic event.

Concerning any literary work of narrative nature, some might read the setting as a series of details supplied for purposes of information. A very different function of setting in literary works has been suggested by two literary scholars and theorists, Rene

---

1. An earlier version of this chapter, "*Ma'amad Har Sinai*: The Hasidic Homilist and the 'World of History,'" appeared in *Hebrew Studies*, Vol. 45 (2004) 193–210.

Wellek and Austin Warren.[2] The details of a setting, in their view, are presented neither for informational nor decorative purposes but rather for their symbolic and metaphorical import.

The Hasidic homilists read such elements in the biblical description of the setting of *ma'amad har Sinai* as emphatically symbolic in import. But in their homilies, unlike in examples cited by Warren and Wellek, the elements of the setting often go beyond any direct relationship to the event being described. As heirs of the tradition of rabbinic midrash, interpretations in the Hasidic homilies at times view such details as independent of the context of the chapter or of the particular verse—in this case as independent of the particular scene and episode of the Sinaitic Revelation. This literary phenomenon recalls the observation of Yitzhak Heinemann concerning the tendency of rabbinic lore (*agada*) to grasp any detail in a biblical verse as inviting interpretation without reference to a central or semantic meaning of the verse or passage as a whole.[3]

In the Hasidic homilies, for example, the fire upon the mountain is understood as conveying intensity and passion in a person's inner devotion, a reading of such elements concerning the physical setting in the biblical text in terms of a landscape of the inner life. Various elements of the setting, it becomes evident, are viewed not as an elucidation of what once occurred at a particular event or point-in-time, but rather as symbolic of what can recur at any point of time, transcending the very scene and event being described.

Examples abound. Elimelekh of Lyzhansk, as we have already noted, overheard in the setting of the desert in the biblical account an allusion to a profound solitude which allows for the devotee's inner attachment to the Divine. To Elimelekh's mind any reference to the desert might be read as an allusion to *hitbod'dut*, a prayerful solitude which contrasts with the symbolic understanding of *Mitzrayim* (Egypt) as a space dominated by shells (*k'lipot*) of

2. Wellek and Warren, *Theory of Literature*, 188.

3. Heinemann, *Darkhe ha-Aggadah*, 78, 96–97, 101. Also Handelman, *The Slayers of Moses*, 78.

impurity. The same homilist read the coming of the Israelites to the Wilderness of Sinai as their turning away from pursuing the futile vanities of the world to a very different life marked by solitude and contemplation. Geography is rendered insignificant as anywhere one can make that transition within one's own inner life from the demonic and impure, oriented to what is external, to a solitude in which a person relates to the depth within the self where one discovers a connection with God.[4]

Drawing upon an older source that refers to the *Shekhinah* (the Divine Presence) as a mountain,[5] Elimelekh read Israel's encamping opposite the mountain (Exod 19:1) as their situating themselves within proximity of the Divine Presence which then shines upon them. A geographical location of the terrain becomes instead a spiritual compass, a statement of the people's mindset being illumined by the light of the Divine.[6]

And in a quite dissimilar vein, the mountain is said to refer to the Evil Inclination (*yetzer hara*), which in a talmudic source[7] is likened to a high mountain, difficult to conquer. Israel's encampment at Sinai as one person, as conveyed in a rabbinic reading of the words "and Israel encamped" (Exod 19:2, employing the singular form of the verb)[8] is read as suggesting Israel's acquiring an inner, moral strength in the face of the ever-present gravitational pull of the Evil Inclination, which is as strong as a high mountain.[9] Building upon an association of a mountain with the quality of Judgment,[10] Moses' scaling the mountain becomes a metaphor for overcoming the hardness and solidity of judgment and transforming it to compassion, a function often attributed, in Hasidic lore and teaching, to the Hasidic holy man.

---

4. *No'am Elimelekh (Yitro)*, 154 on Exod 19:1.

5. See Zohar II, 78b, based on Ps 18:10.

6. *No'am Elimelekh*, 154.

7. *b. Sukk.* 52b.

8. *Meh.* on Exod 19:2, 62a.

9. *No'am Elimelekh*, 156.

10. *b. Baba Bat.* 10a.

At the same time, the homiletical comments of Elimelekh of Lyzhansk read Moses' ascent up the mountain as a path to higher spiritual levels and his rising above all blemish. The mountain becomes a ladder which the *tzaddikim* ascend step by step during their journey in life, as God declares, "And I brought you *to Me*" (Exod 19:4). The spiritual ascent of a *tzaddik* is assimilated to Moses' ascent upon Mount Sinai which, through the homily, acquires a prototypical character.[11] And the same Hasidic master and homilist, Elimelekh of Lyzhansk, overheard in the increasing volume of the shofar-sound (Exod 19:19) the figure of the *tzaddik* who moves repeatedly from the level on which he is standing to a somewhat higher spiritual level, bringing down an influx of blessing from above.[12]

The resumption of the account of the Revelation-scene at Sinai includes the words, "And bow low from afar . . ." (Exod 24:1). Levi Yitzhak of Berditchev understood the word, "from afar," not as implying a physical, geographical distance separating the mountain from the people, but rather as suggesting a relationship of distance (*riḥuk*) that must complement the quality of *kirvah*, nearness to God. The latter, *kirvah*, relates to Divine Immanence as the Divine Presence fills all the worlds, there being no particle of space or aspect of being where God is not present, while the word, *riḥuk*, suggests the light of the *Ein-sof*, the infinite state of the Divine which is beyond all our concepts and conceptions and transcends all human mental grasp. The one relationship evokes *ahavah* (love) while the other, equally necessary, evokes *yir'ah* (fear, awe and reverence). Both, the Berditchever asserted, have their place in one's spiritual life.[13]

Elimelekh further explained the words, "And they took their places at the foot of the mountain" (Exod 19:17), as referring to the innerness of the Torah, likened to the bottom part of the mountain which is deeper than its surface-view.[14] Curiously, in the same

11. *No'am Elimelekh* (Yitro), 154.

12. Ibid., 157.

13. *K'dushat Levi ha-Shalem* (*Mishpatim*), 139.

14. *No'am Elimelekh* (Yitro), 156.

collection of homiletical comments, *Noʿam Elimelekh*, another passage (on Exod 24:16–17), referring to the Presence of God situated on the mountain-top, is similarly read as referring to the innerness of the Torah, based on the shared consonants of the two words, *shoresh* ("root") and *rosh* ("head or "mountain-top").[15] While those particular images might actually contradict one another, each in its own way attempts to convey the sense that the Torah itself has a dimension of soul and innerness beyond what is immediately evident and accessible.

Levi Yitzhak of Berditchev read the verse, "And the sight of the Divine Presence appeared as a consuming fire in the eyes of the Israelites" (Exod 24:17), as an allusion to the human heart which burns with inner enthusiasm like fire, a sign that God finds delight in that person's serving Him and consequently sends holy thoughts within that person's heart.[16] Again, the description of an external phenomenon is read as a metaphor for an aspect of the inner life. And relating to that scene of the mountain ablaze "to the heart of the heavens" (Deut 4:11), Menahem Nahum of Chernobyl utilized the dual meanings of the word *lev* ("heart") as suggesting God's bringing down to Israel the very qualities associated with the heart: "The mountain burned to the heart of the heavens until (Israel acquired) a heart."[17]

In a remarkable though somewhat complex homily of Kalonymus Kalman Epstein of Krakow[18] on the smoke rising from the mountain which is ablaze (Exod 19:18), the Revelation-scene at Sinai is understood through the analogy with a sacrificial rite. While focusing largely upon physical components of the smoke and its place in sacrifice, the analogy does not hesitate to cross the line separating physical aspects from their symbolic and emotional significance. The suitable kind of white smoke that ascends during a sacrifice, the homilist explained, is brought about by the fire and tears of *t'shuvah*, the sincerity of regret and the profound resolve

15. Ibid.

16. *K'dushat Levi ha-shalem* (*Mishpatim*), *umar'ah*, 142.

17. *Maʾor ʿeinayim* (*Yitro*), 35b.

18. *Maʾor va-Shemesh* on Exod 19:17, part II, (*Yitro*), 19b–20a.

to change. Tears of repentance serve as the key-ingredient of the phenomenon of smoke, and those tears then invite the response of a Divine fire from above that burns the sacrifice: an awakening from below, from the human plane, ignites a Divine response, an awakening from above.

Also in prayer, which corresponds to sacrifice, the homilist explained that it is that same inner fire, those same tears of repentance which render prayer whole and acceptable and which, like a sacrifice offered upon the altar, transform a person's very fat and blood to white, the color of atonement.[19] The preacher explained that it was the inner enthusiasm and longing of the Israelites in their response at Sinai that brought about an identical process producing white smoke upon the mountain. The intensity of the Israelites' spiritual passion evoked an awakening from above in the form of "God's revealing Himself and descending in fire to give (to Israel) the Torah."

In this homily, Kalonymus Kalman Epstein drew heavily from an account of the sacrificial act found in the Zohar,[20] but his homily was also highly innovative in connecting the sacrificial rite with the account of the Giving of the Torah at Sinai. The white smoke (the color-system is based on Isa 1:18) upon the mountain, "like the smoke of a furnace" (Exod 19:18), served as a metaphor for man's depth of devotion and proceeds from an inner, metaphorical fire which transforms the person or the community.

One might suggest that such an analogy between the Sinaitic event and a sacrificial rite subtly and implicitly removes the subject of the Revelation at Sinai from the category of unique one-time happenings, and locates it instead in what is recurrent by nature. The analogy transcribes what is understood as an historical narrative of the Revelation at Sinai into a story of spiritual life whenever and wherever it occurs. The symbolic import of the setting tends to acquire a life of its own in which the very narrative and the unique nature of the event tend to dissolve.

19. *Ma'or va-shemesh*, II (*Yitro*), 20a.
20. Zohar II, 20b.

Words, phrases, and verses relating to the setting are shorn from their narrative context, which refers to what is viewed as a central moment of time, and the text is read as a network of allusions to aspects of the spiritual life, ultimately true of all time.

THE MEANING OF DESCENT

In interpreting a narrative found in the Torah, the Hasidic homilist sometimes, in effect, substituted one kind of narrative for another. He overheard in the biblical narrative-account a particular kind of movement that he then identified as the real thrust of the story, and then went on to read that thrust both as independent of the narrative text itself and as transcending the narrative-historical nature of the text.

Chapter 19 of the book of Exodus, for example, is replete with vertical movement—ascending and descending. "On the third day the Lord will come down, in the sight of all the people, on Mount Sinai" (Exod 19:11), "Moses came down from the mountain to the people" (Exod 19:14), "The Lord had came down upon (the mountain) in fire" (Exod 19:18), "The Lord came down upon Mount Sinai, on the top of the mountain, and the Lord called Moses to the summit of the mountain and Moses went up" (Exod 19:20), "The Lord said to Moses, 'Go down, warn the people . . .'" (Exod 19:21), "So the Lord said to him, 'Go down, and come back together with Aaron'" (Exod 19:24), "And Moses went down to the people and spoke to them" (Exod 19:25). In particular, expressions of a *downward* movement reverberate in Hasidic homilies on the scene of the Revelation at Sinai in varying but highly significant ways.

Levi Yitzhak of Berditchev gave emphasis to the seemingly paradoxical nature of the account in which Moses was commanded to go down after having been directed specifically to ascend the mountain. The Berditchever emphasized that Moses had to descend so that the people too might hear the words of Torah which he would relay to them. Furthermore, to the mind of the Berditchever, as we have seen already, Moses was told not to prepare so intensively for the Sinai experience lest afterward, being on a distinctly higher level, he might be "unable to study together with his people."[21] Moses was called to forego the mystic heights he personally experienced and descend to a lower, more limited level, which the multitudes would be able to comprehend.

Implied in Levi Yitzhak's understanding of the command to Moses to descend is the imperative directed not only to the learned scholar—accused of lacking real connection with the members of his community—to retreat from his isolated and erudite heights in the talmudic academy, but also to the mystic who truly fulfills his role only with the ability to relate to the people-at-large whom he must seek to influence and elevate.[22] While Moses attained a much higher level of *d'vekut* (inner attachment with God) than did his people, at his higher level he was incapable of understanding how one could possibly transgress a Divine command, and for this reason it was necessary that he go down so that he might grasp the very need to warn his people.[23]

The Berditchever read the verses of Exodus, ch. 19, as an internal drama within Moses, who was being pulled in two different directions: though preferring to remain on the mountain-heights alone with God, he is commanded instead to go down to the people so that he might communicate with them and teach them. This happening, by implication, then recurs in the case of every *tzaddik* who must similarly, in some sense, descend to a lower level to fulfill his role.

If Levi Yitzhak heard in that verb-root *yrd* ("descend") a sociological message concerning types of religious leadership, to his teacher, the *Maggid*, Dov Baer of Mezhirech, that verb-root suggested a metaphysical meaning. Commenting on the verse, "And the Lord came down upon Mount Sinai, on the summit of the mountain . . ." (Exod 19:20), the *Maggid* heard an allusion that the Divine, ultimately the one, sole, infinite reality, retreats, as it were, from its truer and more sublime nature quite beyond the reach of either human language or thought, to a level accessible to human

---

21. *K'dushat Levi ha-shalem* (*Yitro*), 129, *uMoshe.*

22. See, similarly, Wineman, *The Hasidic Parable*, 118–36.

23. *K'dushat Levi ha-shalem* (*Yitro*), 132, *vayomer.*

understanding with all its limitations. His coming to Sinai to utter His words represents "a descent for God, for though the Divine is infinite, (in that higher state) the worlds are unable to bear (that state of) the Divine."[24]

In Revelation, moreover, not only does God—from a human vantage-point—necessarily retreat from His own infinity beyond all speech and communication, but the Torah also descends insofar as it is revealed in a highly contracted state. In its truer, higher state, the Torah, equated with Divine Intelligence and Wisdom, is infinite, necessarily transcending our own finite and reduced conception as found in the Torah as we are familiar with it.[25] With Revelation, as understood by the *Maggid*, that more sublime state of the Torah assumes a material, historical form, a finite text with a certain number and series of words and letters understood as relating to human existence precisely in this lower, finite, corporeal world.[26] Having undergone contraction (*tzimtsum*), Torah as we know it is the supernal Torah clad in our own type of world.[27] "When the Torah was given at Sinai, it was (already) given in (human) language (in words),"[28] translated into terms of our own physical and finite level of being.

Hasidism's early teachers read the command to Moses to descend (*yrd*, go down) as allusions which transcend its narrative meaning as such. In that key verb-root, the Berditchever and the *Maggid* of Mezhirech each heard, in their respective ways, other levels of meaning relating either to a spiritual teacher's role or to the very nature of man's mental and spiritual life.

---

24. *Rimze Torah*, also known as *Or Torah* (*Yitro*), 40, *vayered*.

25. *Maggid d'varav l'Ya'akov*, #56, 85. Also Theodor-Albeck, *Bereischit rabba*, I, 157, and notes and sources mentioned in Heschel, *God in Search of Man*, 262–63.

26. *Maggid d'varav l'Ya'akov*, #122, 202.

27. Ibid., #134, 234.

28. Ibid., #134, 236.

TIME AND ITS TRANSCENDENCE

In one of his homilies,[29] Menahem Nahum of Chernobyl posed the question: How is it possible to relive events of the past as though they are occurring in the present, initially, for the first time? Referring specifically to the Giving of the Torah, the homilist asked, "Is not the Torah already given?" and then turned to a talmudic saying, frequently cited in Hasidic homilies, that Abraham fulfilled the whole Torah including minute regulations implied in toraitic law.[30] Going further back into time, he spoke even of the Torah having being given to the primordial human couple, though for them, he maintained, it was clad in garments of *skin* (*'or*, with the letter *'ayin*). These questions brought the preacher to his central point of contention, namely that "the essence of the Receiving of the Torah is to be found in the cessation of the (people's) impurity" as a consequence of which they were able to understand the Torah as clad in *light* (*or*, with the letter *aleph*), and the Israelites were then able to perceive the light and the innerness of the Torah.

What has happened to the narrative of the Revelation at Sinai and to its character as belonging to "the world of history?" That narrative, in the light of Menahem Nahum's comment, would refer not to the *giving* of the Torah as such, but rather to Israel's *receiving* the Torah and to the fluctuations in the human ability to grasp the real Torah at different points-in-time. The Torah is always given, was always given; what changed were the obstructions within the human subject, the impurity inherent in the human being stemming from the sin of the primordial couple which did not enable Israel or humankind to grasp the Torah properly, and the overcoming of those obstructions.

Yitzhak of Radvil raised the same objection in terms of philosophical implications of the unity of God, namely the identity of God with His knowledge and will. In his homilies, as they appear in *Or Yitzḥak*, he wrote the following, "There is no element of change

29. *Maʾor ʿeinayim* (*Yitro*), 35a.
30. *b. Yoma*, 28b.

in God's holy will, which is (identical with) God's essence."[31] In that passage, the Radviller denied the possibility of any change within God, viewing any change involving the Divine will—such as God's not having given the Torah until a particular moment of time—as tantamount to a philosophical impossibility. The Radviller confronted "the world of history" and its relation to time on a very different plane of discourse.

The words of the Radviller echo the idea set forth in Maimonides that the proper understanding of the Divine unity makes for an identity of God with His knowledge, so that it may be said that "God is the knowledge, the knower, and the known,"[32] a conception having its roots in ancient Greek thought. Such abstract conceptions, originally relating to the Aristotelian God-concept, were known to Maimonides and to Abraham Abulafia and to the stream of ecstatic Kabbalah[33] and, centuries later, became part of the prism of ideas of the Hasidic homilist.[34] The abstraction of the philosophers colored certain Hasidic comments on the biblical Revelation-scene, mandating an understanding that to a significant degree transcends narrative and even challenges the view of the Revelation at Sinai as a happening bound up with a particular moment of time.

To the mind of the Radviller, to think in terms of God's revealing the Torah at Sinai, revealing what was not revealed prior to the Sinaitic event and not revealed in the same manner after that point-in-time, would posit change within God and within His will.[35] Instead, the voice of God—the homilist asserted—must be understood as above time, as perpetually present, accessible, always sounding, the hearing contingent on man's degree of purification from materiality. God always speaks, but man is not always capable of hearing. It then becomes clear that *ma'amad har*

---

31. *Or Yitzḥak* ('*Eikev*), 187, also (*Yitro*), 129–30.

32. Maimonides, *Mishne Torah*, *Y'sodei ha-Torah* 2:10; also *Sh'monah p'rakim*, ch. 8, and *Yigdal* (*The Authorized* Daily *Prayer Book*, 22).

33. Idel, *Kabbalah—New Perspectives*, 210.

34. Ibid., 242, notes 232–35.

35. *Or Yitzḥak*, 187, comments on *Va'etḥanan* placed within '*Eikev*.

Sinai consists of only one story: that of man's surmounting the barrier to his hearing the Voice which never ceases to address him. Only with spiritual purification could the Israelites hear the Voice amidst the fire.

Sinai, then, is no longer an event of God's disclosing His Will at a central point in time, and the primacy of the moment of Sinai as a singular act of Revelation is removed from the total picture.[36] The same Voice heard at Sinai, the Radviller explained, is perpetually heard, was heard before Creation and is heard today, and while humans might not hear the Voice due to their materiality and their attunement to material and physical desire, in every generation there are righteous and saintly persons capable of hearing that Voice.[37] In this light, Yitzhak of Radvil[38] explained the talmudic agada[39] in which the Messiah explains that he will come "today, if you listen to (God's) voice" (Ps 95:7). As Elimelekh of Lyzhansk had earlier suggested, only after liberating oneself from considerations of self-interest (*p'ni'ot*) is a person able to hear the Divine Voice.[40]

Abstraction entered the picture to impact a tradition's view of its own sacred history and of its central and foundational narrative in a way to nullify the narrative character of the Revelation at Sinai. But perhaps the impact of philosophical abstraction alone does not account for this development. It might flow also from another source which then strangely links up with the kind of abstraction spoken in a Maimonidean language. Already in the nature of rabbinic *agada,* the tendency is noted to a degree to read what is related in the Torah not as a one-time occurrence (*had-pa'ami*), but as something that is essentially or potentially recurrent (*rav-pa'ami*).[41] This tendency became expressive of something

36. Schatz-Uffenheimer, *Hasidism as Mysticism*, 130–31.

37. *Or Yitzḥak* (*'Eikev*), 188. See Wineman, "Hewn from the Divine Quarry," 179–207.

38. *Or Yitzḥak* (*'Eikev*), 188.

39. *b. Sanh.* 98a.

40. *No'am Elimelekh* (*Yitro*), 153–54.

41. Heinemann, *Darkhei ha-Aggadah*, 22, 35.

intrinsic within the Hasidic ethos. It is of the nature of homilies in general that the preacher's actual concern is not with details of the past but with his own present reality and that of his listeners. And the Hasidic homily in its own particular way tended to view any happening recounted in the Torah as potentially and intrinsically recurrent in every present moment.

Similarly the event of Revelation, like much else, is grasped as belonging to all of time. The sense of the biblical text was molded in a way to mirror this basic undercurrent in the consciousness of the Hasidic homilist.

A RE-CONSIDERATION OF TIME

Generalization, however, must be qualified, for the classical Hasidic homilist was also capable, when he felt it important, of relating seriously to narrative and to the world of sacred history.

The reader meets with passages in Hasidic texts which preserve the historical and narrative quality of the toraitic passage intact and firmly anchored to time, place and context. While adding the touches of the homilist to that narrative in a way to mirror his own tenor and temper, such homilies clearly preserve what might be called the latitude and longitude of narrative and relate to the time-oriented sacred history seriously enough both to utilize that narrative and to subtly refashion it.

A striking example can be found in a homily by Efrayim of Sedilikov[42] (whom we will meet more significantly way in the following chapter), which repeated a view found in a rabbinic midrash on Song of Songs[43] conveying the spiritual failure of the Israelites at Sinai. The classical midrashic source identified that failure not with the making of the Golden Calf, as the reader might more readily expect, but rather with the Israelites' request that they might hear the Divine Words not directly from God but rather from the mouth of Moses (Exod 20:19).

42. *Degel maḥaneh Efrayim* (*Yitro*), 111–12.
43. *Midr. Song.*, 1.2.4 on Song 2:1.

Efrayim explained that this request came in the wake of the Israelites' preoccupation with the thunder and fire accompanying the scene of Revelation rather than with the Divine Words themselves, in particular with the very opening word of the Decalogue, *anokhi* ("I"). Consequently, a screen emerged serving as a barrier between the Israelites and God, resulting from their fateful request. In Efrayim's view, that request that Moses, and not God, speak the Words to the Israelites constituted an event of pivotal importance and consequence in sacred history:

> ... for it is known that had the Israelites not said to Moses, "You, speak with us," but had actually heard all the Words instead from the mouth of the blessed Holy One, then the very existence of the Evil Inclination would have been annulled and the people would never, at any time, have come to sin .... [44]

And Efrayim went on to offer an explanation that he attributed to his grandfather, the Ba'al Shem Tov:

> For learning from a holy man is a great thing, and all the more so is learning from the Creator Himself. . . . And certainly the living power of the Master (the Creator) would be felt in the students, for just as He is living and His words live and exist, so it would be the case also concerning the Israelites that those words would live and endure for all time and never cease. Such is not the case, however, when they hear the Words instead from a mouth of flesh and blood.[45]

In perspective, the homily's stance stakes out a position in a kind of protracted debate running through classical midrashic sources concerning the virtue or blemish expressed in that request on the part of the Israelites. While repeating the midrashic comment, critical of the Israelites' request (one with which Rashi's comment on Deut 5:24 concurs), that position directly contradicts a comment included in a still earlier source, *M'khilta de-Rabbi*

---

44. Ibid., 112. Also *Midr. Song.*, 1.2.4 on *Song.* 2:1.

45. Ibid., (*Yitro*), 111–12.

Yishma'el, which understood the people's request to Moses to be highly meritorious and characterized by a "positive shyness."[46]

Furthermore, within the Torah itself, when the same episode of the Israelites' request is retold in Deuteronomy, it is written, *hetivu kol asher dibeiru*, "They did well to speak in this way" (Deut 5:25). Though the Zohar understood the people's reaction as indicating that they were not prepared to ascend to the Tree of Life, that same text nevertheless added that the Torah does not castigate the people for their request insofar as it was made in a devout and reverent spirit.[47] And Efrayim of Sedilikov himself, in another, less forceful homily referring to verses from Deuteronomy, ch. 5,[48] found justification for their request in the Israelites' fear of falling from a higher spiritual level, one based solely on Divine rather than on human initiative.

In his homily criticizing the Israelites' request, Efrayim of Sedilikov maintained a serious relationship with the biblical text as narrative and as sacred history. At the same time, his interest in that sacred history, we might contend, essentially concerned not the past but rather the present. He likely read the past as an analogy to his own hour of history, viewing the failure of the Israelites as an implicit analogy to what eighteenth-century Hasidic teachers generally perceived to be the defects of conventional Jewish religious life in their own time. In their request to Moses, the Israelites sought, in effect, to shield themselves from a direct experience of the Divine. And was not early Hasidism's ultimate indictment of the Jewish religious landscape they knew an accusation that it transformed the Torah-tradition itself into a marvelous structure of intellect capable of shielding Jews from the very experience of the Divine which the *Ḥasidim*, in contrast, felt to be manifest within all the aspects of that very tradition?

With Moses' speaking the Divine Words to the people, those Words are, in some sense, reduced to human words with an innate tendency of becoming severed from spiritual experience.

46. *Meh.*, 72a; II, 272 on Exod 29:16.

47. Zohar, III, 261ab.

48. *Degel Maḥaneh Efrayim* (*Yitro*), 111–12.

The teachers of Hasidism felt that the Torah, though Divine, is nevertheless capable of being severed from the experience and sense of the Divine present in its very letters. Efrayim, more than likely, detected a close connection between the Israelites' request to Moses and the Hasidic critique of much of more conventional religious practice and study as something reduced to the level of behavior "learned from people" (*k'mitzvat anashim m'lumdah*, an expression based on Isa 29:13).

This same contrast is conveyed elsewhere[49] as Efrayim interpreted a talmudic saying that "one who reviews his learning one-hundred times is not like one who reviews it a hundred-and-one times,"[50] explaining that the number *one*, signified by the first letter of the Hebrew alphabet, *aleph*, symbolizes the Master of the Universe. Hence, "studying one's portion a-hundred-and-one times" really means experiencing the Divine as present within one's act of study, within the Torah's very letters. That kind of study, by its very nature, is distant from study which is severed from such experience of the Divine Presence.

Efrayim of Sedilikov drew his understanding of the Israelites' request to Moses as a pivotal failure from a much older midrashic source. But he overheard in that failure of the Israelites at Sinai what was for him a more specifically contemporary nuance: that while God wished the Israelite population to stand at Sinai as *Ḥasidim*, they stood, instead, as *Mitnagdim* (the opponents of Hasidism), living that moment with a preference for the security of distance from the Divine. It is noteworthy that Efrayim omitted the note found in the older midrashic tradition on Song of Songs that the Evil Inclination, which was temporarily removed at Sinai, would be further removed only at a time of future messianic fulfillment: implicit in that omission is the possibility of his viewing Hasidism, with its emphasis upon the experiential, as a potential mending of that failure of the Israelites at Sinai.

Menahem Nahum of Chernobyl had defined the basic significance of *ma'amad har Sinai* as the removal of a basic impurity

49. Ibid., (*Tzav*), 153.

50. *b. Hag.* 9b.

(*zuhamah*) from the Israelites with their willingness to accept the Torah.[51] In older sources,[52] humankind acquired this state of impurity through Eve, and after its removal from the Israelites at Sinai, it was restored soon afterward with their making of the Golden Calf. Earlier sources identified that impurity primarily with lust, while in Hasidic texts the effect of the sin of the first couple is associated also with being attuned to what is external rather than to one's innerness,[53] and also with pride and an egocentric consciousness.[54] According to Yitzhak of Radvil,[55] upon the removal of that impurity, the Israelites could realize that they are of the very essence of God—a new and radical understanding of the self, acquired at Sinai—implying that the lack of that realization itself constitutes their impurity.

Menahem Nahum, however, in his treatment of this older motif of the primordial impurity and its removal, added a further stage with the possibility, even after the Making of the Golden Calf, of gradual, at least partial removal of that primordial impurity through the efforts of those who study Torah in the proper spirit. That impurity could now be removed, not in a single step as had occurred at Sinai, but gradually through time (even though the fullness of restored purification will occur only with messianic fulfillment).[56] Hence, the pattern of sacred history remains incomplete and bestows to followers of any period, including that of the homilist, a role in its unfolding.

Just as the Giving of the Torah at Sinai meant the removal of that primordial impurity so, according to Menahem Nahum of Chernobyl, also after its re-appearance with the Making of the Golden Calf, the act of studying the Torah in a way that seeks its very innerness contributes to removing that impurity. Such study

51. *Ma'or 'einayim* (*Yitro*), 35a–37b.

52. *b. Sabb.* 146a and Zohar, I, 52b; II, 931–94b.

53. *No'am Elimelekh* (*Yitro*), 158.

54. *Ma'or va-shemesh*, part I, 5b (*B'reshit*). Also, *Kol simḥah*, 9 on Gen 3:22.

55. *Or Yitzḥak*, 182 (*l'hag haPesaḥ ha-kadosh*).

56. *Ma'or 'einayim* (*Yitro*), 37a.

makes a dent in the reality of death and evil in the world proportionate to the influx and renewal of the infinite Divine life-vitality (*ḥiyyut*) through the pipelines of Torah.[57] The homily continues with an interpretation of the talmudic saying, "If the Evil Inclination causes you any harm, drag the wretched thing to the House of Study (*l'veit ha-midrash*)."[58] In quoting that saying, the homilist placed the spotlight upon the word *beit* (*bayit*, "house"), a word which he read, along with others, as connoting innerness.

True Torah-study, in line with Hasidism's own character, connects with a strong sense of the innerness of the Torah. It is apparent in those comments that Hasidism, accused and denigrated by its foes for deflating the importance of Torah-study, reclaimed that endeavor for itself and placed its own stamp upon what it viewed as the nature of true and proper Torah-study.

Torah-study in this spirit comprises a miniature *ma'amad har Sinai*, gradually removing the primordial impurity that had earlier been removed and then restored. The inner quality of reverence, Menahem Nahum explained, the required and indispensable preparation for the Giving of the Torah, remains indispensable also for the study of Torah.[59] Moreover, *yir'ah* ("reverence"), it would appear, is akin to the very character of Torah itself, and the proper way of study is precisely to connect with the inner life-force that infuses the letters of the Torah.[60]

It becomes evident, in the above passages, that Hasidism did not always read away narrative and sacred history. In responding to claims made against the Hasidic stream, its homilists provided a serious space precisely for "the world of history" in order, subtly, to refashion that history to provide a significant place within it for the Hasidic thrust itself.

---

57. Ibid., 36b.
58. *b. Kidd.* 30b.
59. *Ma'or 'einayim* (*Yitro*), 35b.
60. Ibid., 37a.

6

Degel Maḥaneh Efrayim
An Ideology of Interpretation[1]

INTERPRETATION AS A DIVINE
REQUIREMENT AND AS A WORLD-VIEW

Many homilists in the Hasidic camp, at least consciously, felt no problem with interpretation and, hence, made no effort to justify the kinds of interpretation which they employed. A rather clear exception would be Moshe Hayyim Efrayim of Sedilikov (c. 1740–1800), a grandson of the Ba'al Shem Tov himself, and a homilist whom the reader will recall from the previous chapter. Efrayim's collected comments on the Torah, *Degel maḥanehEfrayim*, might impress the reader as being remote from an innocent reading of the Torah-text through the author's ideological prism. The work's frequent comments on the subject of interpretation could reveal the need felt by the preacher to justify the gulf separating the *p'shat*, the obvious plain meaning of a verse

1. An earlier version of this chapter, "A Wrestling with Interpretation in a Classical Hasidic Text," appeared in *Conservative Judaism* LXIX.2 (1997) 68–74.

or narrative found in the Torah, from his own interpretations of the same text.

INTERPRETATION AND TIME

Efrayim provided a context for interpretation in what he felt to be the very nature of the world. He envisioned the cosmos as perpetually in the process of an ongoing and renewed Creation, and the preacher would emphasize that lacking that sense of constant re-creation of the world, one becomes spiritually aged and lifeless.[2] He overheard in the words from the traditional morning prayers, "each day, in His goodness, God continually renews the work of Creation,"[3] a connection between the ongoing renewal of all the worlds and an innovative understanding of the Torah, with the claim, in fact, that the very renewal of the world depends upon a constant human endeavor to discover ever-new meanings of the Torah.[4] In the initial commandment of the Torah (Exod 12:2), for example, he heard in the word *ḥodesh* ("month," which begins with the new moon) a clear allusion to *ḥadash* ("new"), and the relationship between the two words sharing the same letters conveyed to his mind not only a justification but a sacred necessity of innovative interpretation.[5] "It is engraved upon the Tablets," he wrote, "that each member of the family of Israel must seek new understanding of the Torah."[6]

To the preacher whose interpretations are collected in *Degel maḥaneh Efrayim*, it is evident that the meaning of the Torah is not static but is, rather, intrinsically related to varying points in time. Efrayim viewed time as consisting of moments and days which are in essence not repetitive but rather unique. "For times are not equivalent, and one day is not similar to the next," and

2. *Degel maḥaneh Efrayim* ('Eikev), 234.
3. *Authorized Daily Prayer Book* (*Shaḥarit*), 108–9.
4. *Degel* (B'reshit), 6–7.
5. Ibid., (*Bo*), 98.
6. Ibid., (*P'kudei*), 146–47.

he interpreted the words, "*This day* I will come to the well" (Gen 24:42) to infer that one can approach the Torah (traditionally associated with the metaphor of a well of water) only in terms of the particular point-in-time in which one stands: as a unique point-in-time, he insisted, each day and each hour of history has its own unique understanding of the Torah.[7] He read the biblical statement that David's old clothes or bed-clothes failed to keep him warm (1 Kgs 1:1) to indicate that older interpretations, which may have spoken to a previous time, are no longer satisfactory and are unable to enliven the spirit.[8] The tenor of his thought would concur with the late Emmanuel Levinas' assertion that real transmission consists not of the petrification of acquired knowledge but rather of invention and renewal.[9]

MAKING THE INCOMPLETE TORAH COMPLETE

Efrayim of Sedilikov referred to the traditional belief that the Written Torah in itself is incomplete—is in effect only half a Torah—without the Oral Tradition of the Rabbis which complemented it and made it whole.[10] He then extended this thought with the claim that each and every generation necessarily receives the Torah in an incomplete state—each generation receiving but half the Torah—and is given the task of making it whole through its own understanding of the text,[11] an understanding that reflects the interpreters and the "soul of the generation."[12]

Each generation, Efrayim continued,[13] has its own unique collective soul which differs from that of any other generation, a

---

7. Ibid., (*Ḥayye Sarah*), 32–33.

8. Ibid., (*Vayetze*), 42.

9. Emmanuel Levinas, quoted in Quaknin, *The Burnt Book*, 15.

10. *Degel* (*B'reshit*), 5–6; (*Sh'mini*), 165.

11. Ibid., (*B'reshit*), 5–6; (*'Eikev*), 241.

12. Ibid., (*Va'era*), 89.

13. Ibid., (*B'reshit*), 5–6.

statement evoking the formula that each generation refracts the Torah tradition through its own soul-root which presumably reflects that generation's total experience and mindset. Efrayim's comments voice the conviction that the bridge to the transcendent, to what is beyond time, can be built only upon one's present moment within time, and that those who construct that bridge must indeed relate seriously to the present.

In Efrayim's view, the present is spiritually as significant as the past "The new meanings which holy men proclaim concerning the Decalogue," Efrayim stated, "are actually on the same level of importance as the words which proceeded from the mouth of God."[14] And even more radical import might be understood in Efrayim's admission that in interpreting the Torah, we actually annul the (plain meaning of the) toraitic verse by means of questions which give rise to multiple meanings, expanding the sense of the verse; these readings are the offspring of the toraitic verse, and insofar as its offspring is alive, the verse itself, though in one sense annulled, is nevertheless alive.[15]

It is quite common, perhaps even normative within the history of religions, that what are in reality new ideas claim to be but a restatement of earlier ideas known already from the beginning or early history of that particular tradition. New concepts and interpretations clad a mask of tradition, and innovation poses as a restatement of an earlier understanding. At any later stage in the development of a religious tradition, adherents tend to identify their own beliefs, values and understandings with the original understanding of the Divinely revealed truth, seemingly negating any space for innovation, and there is no lack of examples of this phenomenon within all religious traditions. In striking contrast to that overriding tendency, Efrayim of Sedilikov, almost amazingly stands out in his clear and conscious recognition of the fact of innovation in interpretation.

14. Ibid., ('*Eikev*), 241.
15. Ibid., (*Va'ethanan*), 231.

THE RELATION OF INTERPRETATION TO SOUL

A revealing insight into Efrayim's thinking might be found in his comment that the different levels of meaning of the Torah (*p'shat, d'rash, remez,* and *sod*) relate to different levels of the soul or psyche as delineated in kabbalistic teaching. The *p'shat* (the simple, surface-meaning) by implication would relate to the most rudimentary level of the soul, a basic awareness and vitality that he viewed as not essentially different in nature from that found also in animal life and the dimension of the psyche most closely bound up with and dependent upon the physical body, while a retreat from the surface meaning of the text corresponds to higher levels of soul.[16] To his way of thinking, the further an interpretation distances itself from a text's literal meaning, the higher the level of soul to which it corresponds. While *p'shat*, it would appear, reflects the limitations of an almost subhuman mentality, readings of the Torah-text that consider the possibilities of allusion, symbolism, and mystery speak to deeper dimensions of the human psyche, extending to the hidden Divine root of the individual soul. "One's level of grasping the Torah," he stated, "is in accordance with the spiritual level on which that person is situated." Furthermore, he explained that a person acquires those various higher dimensions of soul precisely through one's engaging in Torah-study on their corresponding levels.[17]

In his homiletical comments in *Degel maḥaneh Efrayim*, Efrayim of Sedilikov drew upon a host of methodologies of textual interpretation drawn from both midrashic and kabbalistic tradition, strategies allowing for virtually open-ended interpretation. But Efrayim also admitted that the key to the meaning of the text does not actually depend upon such textual strategies, which he considered to be merely means of communication, and at times he fell back on the claim that God sends the interpretation of a verse

16. See Zohar III, 149ab and 152a.

17. *Degel (Ha'azinu)*, 266.

to the interpreter.[18] Interpretation, he would insist, is not reducible to a mental exercise; rather, it is God who enlightens the eyes of the wise to the Torah's meaning.[19]

Efrayim's rationales for interpretation include, perhaps paradoxically, the implications of the eternity of the Torah, a concept which he converts to the premise that the Torah is eternally relevant. Its narratives and laws must be read as relating to every person of any era, its words applicable to all times. A toraitic story necessarily contains "secrets of the Torah which relate to every person and to every era,"[20] and, like non-narrative portions of the Torah, is read largely in terms of allusions that the words suggest to the reader. The meaning of a passage from the Torah cannot legitimately relate solely to a past condition—such as the reality of cultic worship—distinct from the realities of a later time. Rather, it must be possible to fulfill the meaning of any part of the text in terms of the experience and given reality of any and every generation. Such a premise not only explains but actually mandates interpretation.

As an example, it would be contrary to the nature of Torah to read the words relating to the construction of the Tabernacle (*Mishkan*) and its artifacts merely as a set of building instructions; the Tabernacle, after all, was built many centuries ago. Rather, the same detailed instructions must be read, instead, as an imperative to each person to prepare a Tabernacle—a dwelling-place—for the Divine Presence within one's very own self.[21] The interpreter's role, according to Efrayim, is to reveal something of a primordial brightness which is present, even though hidden, within the Torah-text, a light found not necessarily on the surface-level but rather on a deeper level identical with the very soul of the Torah.[22]

Discussing the words, "the Torah which I command you this day is not too wondrous *for you*" (Deut 30:11), Efrayim read the

18. Ibid., (*Mattot*), 230; (*Ḥukkat*), 207–8.

19. Ibid., (*B'reshit*), 5–6.

20. Ibid., (*Lekh l'kha*), 12.

21. Ibid., (*Ki Tissa*), 131–32. Also Wineman, "Sufis in the Hasidic *Mishkan*."

22. Ibid., (*Ki Tavo*), *haftarah*, 259. Note also Zohar, I, 140a.

word *mimkha* as *"through you* or *from you,* meaning that the Torah is not interpreted *other than through you,* and it is only *through you* that the Torah achieves wholeness in its interpretation."[23] In many places in his homilies, Efrayim touched upon the thought that the Torah is not something totally independent of the interpreter, but rather that they interrelate and in a spiritual sense embody one another. Efrayim's ultimate rationale for interpretation underlying *Degel maḥaneh Efrayim* might be summarized by his requirement that an interpreter's understanding of the Torah mirror both the innermost dimensions of his own soul and that of his generation and that, furthermore, it must mirror soulfulness itself.

Though very different from what the stream of Hasidism became over time, that very affirmation of new interpretation has a broader context in an emphasis, found in earlier Hasidic teaching, upon the uniqueness, and hence the newness, of every point in time, the antithesis of experiencing life and time as repetition. This thought is given many different expressions in classical Hasidic texts, and in defining the meaning of prayer Efrayim of Sedilikov spoke of the need for a person to see oneself each morning as a new creation and to perceive all the worlds as new.[24]

It is clear that Efrayim identified the interpretations found in his and other Hasidic homily-texts of his time with an understanding of the Torah rooted in a sense of the uniqueness of his hour of time.

THE SMALL LETTER WILL BECOME LARGE

In explaining the small letter, *aleph,* in the opening word of the third book of the Torah (Lev 1:1) a verse which later mentions the name of Moses, Efrayim explained that in the days of Moses, the Torah itself was small in the sense that Moses himself really understood it only on the level of a passing shadow, "but in the future, God will enlighten us and the holy Torah will be revealed in

23. Ibid., (*Nitzavim*), 260.

24. Ibid., (*'Eikev*) 234–35; note also *Divre Sh'lomo* (*P'kudei ufarshanut haḥodesh*), 107.

the light of the countenance of the King of Life, and then the Torah will itself become much larger, and that small *aleph* will then be written as a large letter . . . ."[25]

25. Ibid., (*Vayikra*), 14.

7

A Hasidic Myth on the Death of Moses and Its Metamorphoses[1]

The Torah (Pentateuch) concludes with the death of Moses (Deut 34). We read that he dies, at the age of one-hundred-twenty years, as a fulfillment of a Divine decree, and he is refused his one request that he be able to live to cross over the River Jordan and enter into the Land to which he had been leading his people over the course of four decades (Deut 3:2–13). Questions relating to that decree and the attempt to understand it evoked an exceedingly interesting discussion in certain passages in the classic Hasidic homily-texts.

Those passages build upon certain themes and comments from earlier texts but tend not to emphasize Moses' punishment for striking the rock as found in the biblical narrative (Num 20:2–13). Instead they relate to Moses' motivation for his request which they explain as being related to an intention on his part to perform, at a precise location in the Land, an act or actions that would bring about complete and ultimate Redemption of his people and a complete repair and unification of all existence.

---

1. An earlier version of this chapter appeared in *Hebrew Studies*, Vol. 54 (2013) 121–32.

In diverse versions, Moses sought to accomplish his goal either by personally fulfilling the *mitzvot hat'luyot ba'aretz* (those commandments of the Torah which can be fulfilled only in the Land of Israel), by pronouncing, at the pre-designated Temple-site, the Ineffable Name in its written form, and/or by his gathering together all the remaining unredeemed fallen Divine Sparks that, in the kabbalistic world-view, were scattered with the *sh'virah,* the primordial cosmic cataclysm which left its severe effects upon all existence.

It is presumed, in those texts, that Moses would have had the potential to completely annul the existence of evil. Moses, however, is not allowed to fulfill that role, either because he had once failed what was a real opportunity, and/or because he could do so only together with the generation which he brought out from Egypt but which had meanwhile perished in the wilderness, or because his fulfilling his role in that way would run counter to the Divine will and wisdom. Due to any of those explanations, the door to such Redemption through Moses during his somewhat extended lifetime was closed.

What is the source of such a conception?

One might perhaps locate the very kernel from which this theme of God's barring Moses from his intended redemptive actions evolved in a classical midrashic text on the book of Lamentations. A *p'tiḥta* of *Midrash Ekha rabbah* includes an involved fantasy-scenario set following the Destruction of Jerusalem and the beginning of the Babylonian Exile. In that scenario Moses, among other biblical figures, is awakened from his grave and informs the prophet, Jeremiah, that he will go with him to bring the exiles out of their distress. Countering all difficulties, Moses, followed by Jeremiah, then made their way as far as the rivers of Babylon. Though the exiles realized that Moses, son of Amram, had actually left his grave to redeem them from their captors, a heavenly voice (*bat-kol*) then proclaimed that "It is a decree from Me." Moses then explained that since God had already decreed the Exile, it is not possible for him to restore the exiles to their land (though he consoled them with the promise that God will quickly restore them).[2]

If the Hasidic tradition mentioned above developed from that midrashic passage, the Hasidic homilies transferred the time of Moses' intended redemptive action from the onset of the Babylonian Exile, centuries after his own lifetime, to the very concluding phase of his own life-span.

In what are probably its earlier Hasidic renditions, following his death Moses is granted a continuing presence in this world through the *tzaddikim*, the righteous, holy men of all the generations, a conception found already in some earlier kabbalistic texts. In different versions, his return in this sense occurs either through *gilgul* (metempsychosis, the soul's entering a person of a later generation from birth) or *ibbur* (soul-impregnation for a limited time at any point during the course of one's life).[3] Renditions of this myth read Moses' post-mortem destiny into the Torah-text itself through their interpretations of two words, *biglalkhem* (Deut 1:37) and *vayit'abber* (Deut 3:26) having a rather vague sound-similarity to the two words, *gilgul* and *ibbur*. And the earlier and more complete renditions of this myth in Hasidic homily-texts make the connection that Moses' death before he could have crossed the Jordan to enter the Land with his people was necessary to allow for his later continuing presence over many generations.

THE MYTH AS PRESENTED IN *NO'AM ELIMELEKH*

A passage from *No'am Elimelekh*,[4] presumably the earliest of the available Hasidic texts of this myth, focuses less on the singularity of Moses than on that of the generation of Israelites who left Egypt. Following an evaluation voiced in much earlier sources, Elimelekh of Lyzhansk (d. 1787) viewed that generation as comprising a

---

2. *Midr. Lam.*, 12a-14b.

3. Scholem, *Kabbalah*, 344–49.

4. *No'am Elimelekh* (*D'varim*), 314–15.

dor de'ah ("a generation of higher spiritual understanding")[5] that would have had the capacity to completely transform evil into good and repair all existence. Within the world of medieval kabbalistic teaching, *Da'at* emerged from a partial fusion of aspects of two *sefirot*, *Hokhmah* and *Binah*. Later, Moses came to be viewed as personifying that quality of *Da'at* which, in Hasidic sources, is identified with spiritual understanding and awareness.

According to Elimelekh's explanation, had that generation, which had gone forth from Egypt and received the Torah from God at Sinai, gone ahead to enter into the Land of Israel as originally intended, Israel would never again have experienced exile; however, with its failure, that unique opportunity to "sweeten the judgments," defeating the forces of evil at their very root, was lost, and the generation which followed and which did enter into the Land did not measure up to the spiritual level of the generation that preceded it. Moses' inability to attain Redemption without his original generation might possibly echo, to a degree, a Hasidic emphasis upon an essential interdependence of the *tzaddik* ("holy man") and his community of followers.

Drawing from the very diverse evaluations of the Generation of the Wilderness found in a talmudic discussion[6] on the statement, in Mishna Sanhedrin, that *dor ha-midbar ein lahem ḥelek ba'olam ha-ba* ("the Generation of the Wilderness have no portion in the World-to-Come"),[7] Elimelekh completely turned that statement on its head to view that generation as uniquely exalted in holiness and virtue.

It would thus appear, in Elimelekh's homily, that Moses had to die in the wilderness (outside the Land) just like his generation through no real fault of his own. Were he allowed to enter the Land, he would have proceeded to fulfill all the commandments of the Torah, including those applicable only in the Land (*hamitzvot*

---

5. *Midr. Lev.*, 9.1; *Midr. Eccl.*, on Eccl. 7:23, and *Pesiq. Rab Kah*, ed. Mandelbaum, 4.3.

6. *b. Sanh.* 110b.

7. *m. Sanh.* 10.3.

hat'luyot ba'aretz),[8] and would have brought his mission to total completion. But his death prior to doing so, hence leaving his work incomplete, was necessary to enable—and to require—his soul to return to the world through metempsychosis (*gilgul*) in the souls of *tzaddikim* (righteous, holy men like himself) who study Torah "for its own sake." Through them, gradually, he could fulfill his more comprehensive role of "sweetening the judgments," combating the very existence of evil and exile. The Righteous of the Generations distinctly parallel the homilist's conception of the Generation of the Wilderness as having valiantly fought in a holy, cosmic war through their devotion to Torah-study out of a pure, unblemished motivation.

Elimelekh drew upon passages in *Tikkunei ha-zohar*, a later layer of zoharic literature, which refer to Moses' influence "extending through every generation, in every *tzaddik*,"[9] and he wove that earlier theme of Moses' *gilgul* into a larger narrative-conception in which Moses' incarnation in such *tzaddikim* is set in motion by the failure of his potentially messianic aspiration during his own lifetime. The dimensions of myth provide the space for Moses to pursue his goal of Redemption instead through a more difficult roadmap encompassing many generations.

Throughout *No'am Elimelekh*, the master and preacher frequently explained the name, Moses, when it occurs in the Torah-text, as referring to "the *tzaddikim*," and in the passage under discussion, he asserted that "the *tzaddik* is called Moses." He also explained that the *tzaddik* has the power to "sweeten the judgments," though in a more limited measure, precisely due "to his study and engaging in Torah *lishmah* (for its own sake, free of any thought of personal advantage),"[10] echoing a key-aspect of the Hasidic polemic directed against the more conventional religious leadership and elite. While, as in the earlier kabbalistic sources, the word *tzaddikim* (literally: "righteous") has a much broader mean-

---

8. *b. Sotah* 14b and *Yalkut Shim'oni*, I, #816. Also, *Kol Simḥah*, 106 (*Va'etḥanan*).

9. *Tikkunei ha-Zohar*, 112a–114a.

10. *No'am Elimelekh* (*D'varim*), 315.

ing, this discourse of Elimelekh, whose homilies focus, to a large degree, on the role of the central figure in a Hasidic community, specifically implies an identification of Moses' continuing presence and redemptive activity through time with the Hasidic mode of study and with Hasidism itself and its spiritual leadership.

Though not quoted in the homily, Elimelekh would certainly have noted, within the talmudic comments on *dor ha-midbar* (the Generation of the Wilderness) mentioned above, the word *ḥasidai* ("My devotees," Ps 50:5), which Joshua ben Karha then understood as referring to "the righteous (*tzaddikim*) in every generation."[11] Both the words *tzaddikim* and *ḥasidai* ("My devotees") would have acquired much more concrete connotations with the appearance of eighteenth-century Hasidism. The idealization of that Generation of the Wilderness as a *dor de'ah* (a generation marked by spiritual understanding) served Elimelekh as an implied analogy of the mystics and teachers around which the various Hasidic communities emerged in his own time.

MYTHIC ASPECTS OF THE PASSAGE FROM *NO'AM ELIMELEKH*

Before proceeding to a few other Hasidic renditions of the themes of Moses' messianic intent and of God's refusal to alter the death-decree for Moses, we might consider some broader mythic themes and qualities reflected in this homily of Elimelekh of Lyzhansk.

The reader might well overhear in the background of this myth a parallel of both Moses and the Messiah with the First Man (*Adam ha-rishon*) whose soul, it is said, encompassed all souls. That midrashic motif concerning the First Man[12] received further emphasis in Lurianic teaching,[13] which extended the same motif also to Moses[14] and which Hasidic homily-texts further extended

---

11. *b. Sanh.*, 110b.

12. *Tanh.* (*Ki Tissa*), #12 and *Midr. Exod.*, 40.3. See Ginzberg, *Legends*, V, 75.

13. L. Fine, *Physician of the Soul*, 143–44.

14. Ibid., 314–15 and n.35 on p. 438. Also note Zohar, I, 28a.

to the Messiah as well. (We will meet this concept further in our final chapter.) Menahem Nahum of Chernobyl explained that "every person who truthfully serves the blessed Creator must contribute that aspect of himself that is his own portion of the Messiah, as is known from the word *adam* ('human,' *alef—dalet—mem*), which consists of the first letters of the names, Adam, David, and *Mashiʾaḥ* (Messiah), and every single person must contribute his own particular quality and portion to reconstitute the totality of the First Man as it existed before his Sin." In this way, the soul of each Israelite will then be included in the Messiah, and as each person's soul was part of the soul of the First Man, so a part of the First Man—and by implication also of the Messiah—is present within each person.[15]

That conception of the inclusion of all Israelite souls within Moses' soul is easily transposed in the claim that something of Moses' soul and essence is present in every *tzaddik* or student and interpreter of Torah in every generation.[16] Or, as expressed by Zeʾev Wolf of Zhitomir (d. 1800) in *Or ha-Meʾir* (which we will also discuss more deeply in our concluding chapter), the aspect of *Daʿat*, which came to be specifically identified with Moses, is understood as the spiritual impulse within the consciousness of every Israelite or even *bekhol adam*, in every person: anyone who has *daʿat kono*, an awareness of relationship with a higher, Divine reality, can on some serious level be referred to as Moses.[17] Such conceptions are akin to the way in which Elimelekh of Lyzhansk viewed the leadership of the stream with which he identified as a collective manifestation of the soul of Moses.

To those who referred to Moses' continued presence after his death, Moses became their own story. That conception sought to explain themselves, their spiritual life and consciousness as Moses, in some important sense, having become the *tzaddikim,* infusing

15. *Maʾor ʿeinayim* (*Shʾmot*), 28b.

16. *Degel maḥaneh Efrayim* (*Shʾmini*), 165.

17. *Or haMeʾir*, I, 135 (*Bʾshalaḥ*), I, 145 (*Yitro*), and 227 (*Tzav*), II, 187–88 (*Vaʾethanan*). Note also *Degel maḥaneh Efrayim* (*Yitro*), 109 and *Maʾor ʿeinayim* (*Shʾmot*), 29b.

their very being. And precisely because of his earlier failure and death, something of Moses' very soul lives in every *tzaddik* of every generation. One can easily grasp the importance of claiming such a mythic identity with Moses for a struggling and even persecuted pietistic stream in the face of fierce and bitter opposition and criticism.

Furthermore, in positing such a paradoxical relationship in the requirement of Moses' death to allow for his continuing presence and for the fulfillment of his intent through time, the basic pattern of this myth molded certain earlier strands to reflect a much broader and older mythic thrust, a paradoxical interdependence of life and death in a way that death contains within it the very seed of life's renewal.

Students of myth and mythology have suggested that such a thematic thrust grew out of human experience from the very beginning of agricultural cultivation in the Neolithic era, as humans observed not only that the life of the field languishes and then revives, but that from the seed, buried in the ground, a new yield of the field eventually grows and sustains life.[18] This theme, underlying a multitude of myths, beliefs, and rites associated with seasonal, agricultural festivals received perhaps its most concise statement in the well-known verse from the Gospel of John, "Unless a grain of wheat falls into the earth and dies, it remains alone; but if it dies, it bears much fruit" (John 12:24), and also in the words from the Pauline writings, "What you sow does not come to life until it dies" (1 Cor 15:36. Note the same image in *b. Sanh.* 90b and in Zohar II, 148b-49a).[19]

Our myth, in the form found in *No'am Elimelekh*, assigns to Moses' death the equivalence of the "buried wheat" deemed necessary for renewal and regeneration. The death and failure of Moses in his own time were necessary to allow for the very possibility of his continued presence throughout the generations in which he

18. Eliade, *Myths, Dreams and Mysteries*, 188–89. Also Frazer, *The Golden Bough*, V-VI.

19. Translation is from the *Revised Standard Version of the New Testament* (Thomas Nelson & Sons, 1946).

represents, in effect, an alternative and essentially different road to Redemption. The implications of this theme identify the Hasidic holy men (*tzaddikim*) as bearing within them something of Moses himself.

The Hasidic homilist wove together a complex network of strands from earlier Jewish sources in a way that reflects that much older and deeply-rooted mythic pattern. While some might presume Christian influence in this myth of Moses' death, the myth's basic pattern itself antecedes Christianity, extending far beyond it.

THE RENDITION IN *MA'OR 'EINAYIM*

Though following the general pattern of the account in *No'am Elimelekh*, a homily of Menahem Nahum of Chernobyl (d. 1787) in *Ma'or 'einayim*[20] locates Moses' failure in his total preoccupation with his people's distress in Egypt. At that time, when his own generation was still alive, he was unable to give any concern whatsoever to the future exiles, which, in kabbalistic teaching, would similarly occur for the purpose of lifting up those Sparks and souls that fell in the wake of the Sin of the First Man. Due to Moses' complete focus on the immediate exile, he bypassed the opportunity that he would have had to gather those fallen sparks in a way that no future exiles would be necessary. That explanation of Moses' failure allows one to grasp the extension of Moses' presence over many generations as a reverse-mirror of Moses' more limited preoccupation with his particular hour of time and its distress.

Menahem Nahum explained the difference between the Generation of the Wilderness and the generation that followed and that went on to enter the Land in that the prior generation served God out of love "as sons," with no concern with reward, whereas the following generation, in contrast, served God "as servants," motivated by expectation of reward.[21] Hasidic homily-texts from its earlier period tend to suggest that the same basic distinction

20. *Ma'or 'einayim* (*Va'ethanan*), 64b–65a.

21. Note *m. Abot* 1.3 and Maimonides, *Mishneh torah, Hilkhot t'shuvah*, ch. 10.

defined the difference between themselves and their opponents, an assertion that implies a rather clear parallel of the Hasidic stream in the preacher's own time with what the master viewed as the *dor de'ah* (a generation marked by spiritual understanding) of the biblical wilderness-period.

In Menahem Nahum's rendition, Moses' failure to realize his aspiration in his own life-span allowed for the granting of a soul-spark of Moses' own soul through *ibbur* to the *tzaddikim* of all the generations. The preacher very clearly situated the extended time of the present and its mode of redemptive activity between Moses' failed messianic aspiration in the past and a future messianic fulfillment in which the Messiah will bear the soul of Moses.

The Chernobyl master considered that the eventual messianic fulfillment is made possible by that extended middle period in which Moses, through the *tzaddikim* of all the generations and their devotion to Torah-study and piety, seeks very gradually to accomplish the *tikkun* (repair) that he failed to achieve alone in his lifetime. Any more overt or external expression of messianism brought about through the act of a single person—it would follow—is deemed irrelevant for the present eon.

A SUBSEQUENT METAMORPHOSIS OF THE MYTH

The myth, as presented in the two texts discussed above, underwent further drastic change in versions that pointed in the direction of a contrast between Moses and the *tzaddikim* of the generations. The homilies of Kalonymus Kalman Epstein of Krakow (d. 1823) and Avraham Yehoshua Heschel of Apt/Opatow (d. 1825), both students of Elimelekh of Lyzhansk, each open with a somewhat different rendition of the nature of Moses' request and of his particular strategy involved in that request.

In *Ma'or va-shemesh*,[22] Kalonymus Kalman explained Moses' insistence upon entering the Land as his intent to effect there a

---

22. *Ma'or va-shemesh*, part 5, 6ab.

unification (*yiḥud*) of the Divine Names by pronouncing the Ineffable Divine Name in its written form.[23] (Normally, according to Jewish law, it is forbidden to pronounce that Divine Name in its written form.) Moses, however, believed that unifying the Divine Names (pronouncing the Ineffable Name as it is written) would have the effect of unifying all the worlds "from the lowest point on earth to the infinite state of the Divine," lifting all the forces of judgments to their higher Source and hence fully realizing the conception of the Oneness of God. While the homilist assumed that Moses might have been able to accomplish that goal, the Krakow preacher informed his followers that Moses' intent was not in accord with God's will for that time.

The homily in *Ma'or va-shemesh* makes no mention of the presence of Moses' soul in the *tzaddikim* through the generations. Instead, it focuses upon Moses' own failure to grasp the truer nature of Exile and Redemption. It defines the very essence of national and cosmic Exile as the illusion that the world, including the workings of nature, thought of principally as everyday existence involving the necessary pursuit of material needs and physical action, is severed from God. Kalonymus Kalman, in that sense, defined the true nature of Exile as essentially psychological in nature. It is a rather specific mindset, a way of thinking that distances the Divine Presence from the world, something that is theoretically impossible insofar as *leit atar panui minei*, "there is no place empty of the Divine"[24] and "His presence fills the world."[25] The Krakow preacher identified that very mindset, which he contended was growing in his own time, as the real impediment in the way of a Unification of all being. Moses' plan of action, accordingly, would be quite irrelevant to the actual nature of Exile.

---

23. Note *Pirque R. El.* (ch. 40, end) and *Midr. Gen.*, 97.6. Also *Sipre* (#28) on Deut 3:25, *b. Sotah*, 38b, *b. Yoma* 39b and *b. Pesah.*, 50a, *Yalqut*, I, #816 and Scholem, *Sabbatai Sevi*, 142, 393, 397–98 and 402–3.

24. *Tikkunei Zohar*, #57, 91b, an Aramaic version of a phrase found in *Midr. Exod.* 2.5.

25. Isa 6:3.

Kalonymus Kalman claimed that, in contrast to Moses' understanding, the *tzaddikim* bring holiness into all aspects of everyday reality and are attached to the *Ein sof* (the infinite, boundless state of the Divine) even while engaging in life's physical and material actions. Their relationship to God impacts the entire scene of life as they seek to reforge a unification of the worlds in the face of the presumption of a disconnect between God and nature. The way of the *tzaddikim* directs one to locate the Divine even within the world of "lowly" (worldly) everyday concerns and to relate the totality of life to God. It seeks to serve God in all that one does in every realm of life in connection with all of one's tasks, responsibilities, and concerns.

To the mind of Kalonymus Kalman, a deep cleavage separated Moses' sense of redemptive activity from that of the *tzaddikim*. He claimed that Moses, who had sought to attain Redemption through his own redemptive actions of a cultic and talismanic nature, misunderstood both the deeper nature of Exile and the path of its undoing. Redemption can be attained or advanced not through a redemptive cultic act of a single individual at a single moment of time, but rather through the *tzaddikim's* very different redemptive path with its very different time-frame.

Echoing Rashi's explanation of the word *va'ethanan* ("and I pleaded," Deut 3:23) as Moses' appealing to God's quality of graciousness (*ḥanun*) rather than making a claim in terms of what Moses deserved, Avraham Y'hoshu'a Heschel of Apt (died, 1825) associated Moses' request with a belief that Redemption can occur through such a gracious and unmerited gift requiring no effort on the part of the recipient, rather than as a result of one's actions and efforts in combating what is evil and unholy. (The same objection is mentioned in a statement by Shneur Zalman of Liady.)[26] Moses' strategy would deprive God of the delight derived through generations of *tzaddikim* who devotedly engage in Torah-study and in fulfilling the *mitzvot* (commandments) even in adverse circumstances. God prefers—the Apt master explained—that the redemption from evil be earned precisely through the devoted

26. *Torah Or* (*Va'ethanan*), 18b.

efforts of an untold number of persons over many generations, whereas Moses' intended action, if carried out, would annul the very purpose of human existence, namely the need for ongoing worshipful living in which adherents reveal the holy that is concealed within their everyday existence and within existence itself. Moses' program for the instant eradication of all evil would annul the very path of the Righteous who struggle with evil, including the evil within themselves, through a life of devotion and service ('*avodah*) to God. And for this reason, the door was closed to Moses' request and his plan.[27]

The reader might sense, up to a certain point, a somewhat parallel strain to the *Apter rebbe's* worldview in the haunting paradox expressed in a parable from Rebbe Nahman of Bratzlav's thirteenth Tale, "The Seven Beggars," which speaks of the heart of the world and its longing for a spring flowing from a rock upon a mountain. It is impossible for the heart of the world to make its way to that spring, yet the continued existence both of the world and of time is claimed to be dependent upon that constant and unfulfilled longing of the heart for the spring, a longing that can never be fulfilled.[28]

THE COMMON ELEMENT IN THE VARIOUS RENDITIONS

The pendulum swung from a striking identification with Moses to a critical view of him. In tracing this series of homilies, the respective teachers and preachers moved from the return of Moses' soul to this world incarnated in the *tzaddikim* of the generations to scenarios that simply omit such a spiritual presence for Moses in the world following his failure and death.

That omission, in turn, goes hand-in-hand with a critical assessment of Moses' intention and strategy as reflecting a basic

27. *Torat emet* (Va'ethanan), 34ab. Note also *b. Hag.* 12a, *No'am Elimelekh* (B'reshit), 21 on Gen 1:3, and *Oheiv Yisra'el* (Va'ethanan), 81ab.

28. *Sefer sippurei ma'asiyot*, 71ab. Tr. Band, *Nahman of Bratslav—The Tales*, 268–69.

misunderstanding on his part. The implicit contrast, present already in the homily of Elimelekh of Lyzhansk, between the messianic actions Moses aspired to accomplish in a single hour of time and the approach of the *tzaddikim* over many generations, deepened to become a critical and explicit divide.

One aspect of the background of this surprisingly critical attitude toward Moses might come into view if one bears in mind that concepts and implications voiced in these particular homilies—the messianic associations attributed to Moses, the unification of Divine Names, as well as the return of Moses' soul manifest in the *tzaddikim* of the generations—all belong to the world of ideas reflected in *Tikkunei ha-zohar* and *Ra'ya m'heimna*, latter strands of the Zoharic literature which also include an antinomian nuance critical of Moses as having understood the Torah solely in legal rather than in deeper, mystic terms.[29] While the various renditions of the refusal of Moses' request in these homilies certainly claim to identify with the tradition of rabbinic learning and law—note the centrality of Torah-study in the characterization of the Generation in the Wilderness and of the later *tzaddikim*—criticisms of that nature voiced in those earlier kabbalistic sources may nevertheless, to a certain extent, have prepared the ground to allow for the kind of critical portrayal of Moses found in the respective homilies of Kalonymus Kalman Epstein and Avraham Yehoshua Heschel of Apt.

The primary factor, however, in the metamorphosis of this tradition, evidently over just a few decades, might be found in Hasidism's improved fortunes. The turn in the relationship to Moses and the omission of the idea that the *tzaddikim* in some sense embody Moses' own soul might be an indication that such mythic grounding for the phenomenon of Hasidism, important for a seemingly marginal stream seeking its place in the Jewish world, became superfluous with the more significant following which it acquired by the early decades of the nineteenth century. Hasidism could stand in its own right without the need to explain itself as a manifestation of the soul of Moses. That earlier identification of

29. Note Giller, *The Enlightened Will Shine*, 65–68.

the *tzaddikim* as a manifestation of Moses' soul gave way to their being identified precisely as a corrective of Moses' own thinking.

Beyond the contrast between the earlier and somewhat later homilies, however, both share in evoking in their listeners an identification precisely with the *tzaddikim* of the generations. The theme of Moses' failure, though variously understood, served as the foreground against which the homilists sought to define themselves and their stream and to provide for them a context in the larger scheme of things. This was the case whether they identified themselves as a spiritual manifestation of Moses or whether they identified themselves in contrast to what they interpreted as the mindset of Moses.

ADDENDUM —IN PERSPECTIVE

To better understand the last two sources discussed, the homiletical legacies of Kalonymus Kalman Epstein of Krakow and Avraham Yehoshua Heschel of Apt, it will be helpful to review the ways in which the writings attributed to each of those two masters relate to Moses more generally.

Ma'or va-shemesh, containing the homilies of Kalonymus Kalman of Krakow, spoke of Moses as a model of humility which explains his hesitation, according to the biblical account, in accepting any kind of leadership role in the struggle to free the Hebrew slaves.[30] And we have already noted above Kalonymus Kalman's reading of Moses' judging the people alone from dawn to dusk as going beyond judgment itself to bring the claimants in a dispute to a true reconciliation and meeting of hearts. While Kalonymus Kalman explained Moses' radiant countenance as the Ineffable Name engraved in his face when he descended from Sinai the second time (Exod 34:29–34), he also seemingly retreated from the uniqueness of that circumstance as he noted that the same has occurred to various persons in the homilist's own time.[31]

---

30. *Ma'or va-shemesh*, part two, 4a.

31. Ibid., part two, 32a.

In addition to the homilist's explanation of God's rejection of Moses' ultimate request, Kalonymus Kalman also indicated, via an animal parable, that Moses' death was seemingly necessary in order that his people might understand that they cannot rely upon any human leader, even upon Moses, to seek forgiveness for their sins. They themselves must atone and seek forgiveness for their transgressions, and only God can forgive them.[32] Though Kalonymus Kalman was responsible for developing a Hasidic presence in Krakow over the course of many years, the reader might easily overhear his warning that each person in a Hasidic community must do one's own spiritual work and not think in terms of the *tzaddik*, the central figure of such a community, as able to do that work for them.

The *Apter rebbe*'s question concerning Moses' understanding should be read, interestingly, in the face of the larger depiction of Moses in that master's teachings.

Echoing earlier motifs revolving around the birth of Moses, such as the light which filled the room when the infant was born,[33] the *Apter rebbe*, Avraham Yehoshua Heschel (d. 1825), made the even bolder claim that Moses "was holy from his birth."[34] Furthermore, extending the narrative of Moses to a cosmic context and its dimensions, Moses' task and endeavor was not limited to bringing his people out from exile and oppression but, in addition, to liberate also a population of angels who were also enslaved there. The nature of the one liberation would be evident, while the deeper exile, involving the Divine world, comprises a liberation beyond the horizon of the visible.[35] His role is explained as nothing less than a liberation of the Points of Holiness from their domination in the Shells (*k'lipot*), a central theme in kabbalistic cosmology.[36]

According to the *Apter rebbe*, Moses was given honor, paradoxically, for the reason that he truly and fully recognized that

32. Ibid., part five, 36a.

33. *Oheiv Yis'rael (Sh'mot)*, 24b.

34. Ibid., (*Sh'mot*), 25a.

35. Ibid., (*Sh'mot*), 25b-26a.

36. Ibid., (*Bo*), 29b.

no one has a claim to such honor or even to think that honor is really his in any sense.[37] On another level, Moses is explained as nothing less than the (human) embodiment of the very mystery of the higher, even supernal, understanding of the Divine Oneness which is to be revealed to the world through him.[38] And as for Moses' worldly knowledge, the Apter master maintained that Moses not only knew the seventy languages of the world's nations but actually translated the Torah into all seventy of them.[39]

What the Hebrews feared at the Reed-Sea, to the mind of the *Apter rebbe*, was not their dangerous situation as they witnessed the approach of the Egyptian chariots, but rather their doubt as to whether they were at all worthy of any Divine action to save them, and Moses gave them encouragement at that crucial moment.[40] In addition, with Moses' Song at the Sea (Exod 15:1–21), all the holy powers and qualities became evident and revealed to the world and were elevated to the level of a Throne, as the Divine role in the universe was made evident for all to witness.[41]

That is not all. The Apter master explained that the true and more ultimate goal of the Exodus was to bring the population he led to an exceedingly higher level in which all aspects of the human body and its desires and external orientation would become subjected to the mind and annulled, and all the thoughts and intentions of humans would be simply to perform the Creator's commanded acts (*mitzvot*), hence doing God's will as they ascend step-by-step from one level to the next higher level. All that comprises the human person will then ascend to a state of virtual self-cancellation as humans would understand their very being in the context of the infinitely higher Divine Presence. In this way they would actualize the very goal of Creation, defined as *ayin*, a mystic negation of any sense of one's very being. And Moses—the *Apter rebbe* informs us—was himself, at all times, on

37. Ibid., (*Sh'mot*), 27a.
38. Ibid., (*Bo*), 28a.
39. Ibid., (*B'shalaḥ*), 35a.
40. Ibid., (*Bo*), 32b.
41. Ibid., (*B'shalaḥ*), 33a.

that exceedingly high level of spiritual consciousness. The ultimate purpose of Creation itself is to bring a person such as Moses into being, one whose very leadership was itself drawn from his exceedingly humble state-of-mind and from the level of his mystic consciousness.[42]

In the comments of the *Apter rebbe*, Moses himself is described as the very source and root of good and holiness themselves, and furthermore—and this is highly significant—he approached all of his deeds and efforts with no expectation or thought of reward as he sought nothing less than to remove all evil itself during the course of his own lifetime.[43]

This ever-so-laudable and hallowed picture of Moses meets, however, God's refusal to allow Moses to live to enter into the Land with his people, an insistence that would clearly call for explanation on the part of the preacher and commentator. The *Apter rebbe* explained God's refusal to grant Moses' request in terms of a claim (not necessarily substantiated from the biblical text) that Moses believed that the world is not based on merit and reward but rather purely on graciousness on God's part, and that due to his own intention rooted in this understanding, Moses had to die and not enter the Land with his people.

Moses' imputed belief in God's graciousness extending beyond a need for humankind's worthy actions and behavior contradicts a strain prevalent throughout the commentaries of the *Apter rebbe*—namely the belief that, with only certain glaring exceptions, an "awakening from above" is dependent upon an "awakening from below."[44] Divine Revelation and its contents would be meaningless unless the human mind and psyche first prepare the ground for their reception in terms of their own ways of thinking which are cultivated over time. And, similarly, Divine blessings

---

42. Ibid., 33b.

43. Ibid., (*Vaethanan*) 81a. In the Apter rebbe's reading of Moses' striking the rock (Num 20:1–13), Moses erred, but with the most holy intention (*Torat emet, Hukkat*, 30a–31b).

44. Note *Oheiv Yisra'el* (*Bo*) 32b, (*Mishpatim*) 38a, (*Vaethanan*) 81a, and (*'Eikev*) 83a.

occur only when humans first prepare the way for them; hence, human acts of lovingkindness must occur before God displays mercy toward the world. The reader might well overhear a rational impulse in this principle which is sounded repeatedly in the *Apter rebbe's* comments—a principle that would run counter to the view that he ascribed to Moses for whom God's graciousness required no prior worthiness on the part of humankind.

Moses' request and God's refusal of that request comprise the dramatic high-point of the *Apter rebbe's* entire homiletical commentary on the Torah. Even with all the marvelous merits and even the cosmic accomplishment which the preacher attributed to Moses, the *Apter rebbe* here made of Moses nothing less than a tragic hero with a fatal flaw.

The commentator, whose words placed Moses on the highest pedestal, appears, in certain places, to have agreed that Moses—were he allowed to enter into the Land—would, in a single act, have been able to eradicate evil itself from the world and the worlds. But at the same time, Moses' act would meet with disapproval from God who thinks in very different terms.

In the eyes of the preacher and commentator, Moses, approaching his death, even with all his accomplishments, meets with a radically different view of reality that goes against the grain of his seemingly noble-intended action. While Moses wished to live in order to enter the Land and there perform his cultic deed eliminating the very nature and existence of evil, God judges Moses' program with its easy path to bring existence itself to perfection to be intrinsically unacceptable. God—and the *Apter* master—think in terms of a more difficult but more meaningful road, a still higher mountain which humankind must climb over the course of countless generations.

In his interpretation of God's refusal of Moses' request, Avraham Yehoshua Heschel of Apt, the *rav* and *rebbe*, homilist and commentator, emerged as a true artist as well. He portrayed Moses in so many ways as a supremely ideal figure, far surpassing and transcending all human norms. Moses' role, as described, is cosmic in its reach and aspirations. Yet, in commenting on God's refusing Moses' request, the *Apter rebbe* inferred that something of Moses' own psyche and understanding suddenly confronts an essentially different sense of reality and of the vaster and more difficult vista of spiritual endeavor.

The reader, furthermore, might decipher within the *Apter rebbe*'s critique of Moses a premonition of a more radical understanding of the presence of evil in the world. In a much earlier and widely accepted view, one that came to be reflected in much of kabbalistic teaching, the very existence of evil is largely ascribed to the Primal Sin on the part of the first human couple. Their sin, in whatever way it is conceived, removed the progenitors of humankind from an angelic existence to one comprising a physical and material nature in which humans are subject to death itself as well as to various impulses, desires, and travails.

The comments of the two Hasidic teachers discussed above might appear to explain evil itself in a very different light. Evil exists not due to some primal misdeed that might be undone, or even to the kabbalistic view of an initial catastrophe (*sh'virah*) in which Divine Sparks became imprisoned in the Shells (*k'lipot*), but rather because only in seriously engaging with evil within the self and the world does humankind day-by-day reveal its true self and spiritual stature. And in God's eyes, such wrestling and engagement with evil is infinitely precious.

In the collections of his homilies, the *Apter rebbe* wrote about Moses in the most laudable terms, even as he expressed a fatal criticism of what he took to be Moses' understanding of the conflict of good and evil. The one does not negate the other: in the eyes of the *Apter rebbe*, Moses remains a holy man in the very highest sense even when his understanding at this point in his biography is subject to criticism. And even the limitation of his understanding does not negate his virtue, as no human, even Moses, has a claim to perfect understanding.

8

Cult and Homily

Moses' role, in terms of the Torah as a whole, is that of a law-giver, a role in which Moses himself is actually an agent of Divine Revelation. The scope of the law attributed to Moses' agency as such encompasses both human ethics and morality, along with what would be considered civil law, and also religious practice that, in the Torah (Pentateuch) itself, centered around the priesthood and sacrificial worship in its various forms, with no firm division between those areas of legislation. All are claimed to be intrinsic parts of the "law of Moses and Israel."

The subject of how the various Hasidic homily-texts of the late eighteenth century and early nineteenth century approached and interpreted the biblical sacrificial cult and its laws, attributed to Divine Revelation through Moses, is of particular interest. A range of attitudes toward the priestly biblical cult can be found in the Hasidic homily-literature, sometimes within the very same texts. And within that literature, various comments point to a definite resistance to understanding the biblical texts on their own terms.

ON THE VERY MEANING OF THE PRIESTHOOD

The classic Hasidic homilists (preachers) strangely felt the need to explain the term *kohen* (priest), as though those whom they were addressing had no understanding or familiarity with the term. And in such cases the definitions offered often overlook or avoid any more obvious understanding of the biblical priesthood.

In *Tol'dot Ya'akov Yosef*, for example, Ya'akov Yosef of Polonnoye—himself a *kohen*—explained the term *kohen* as one who serves God or who loves God.[1] He also read specific laws relating to the *kohanim* as pertaining to *anshei tzurah* and *ba'alei nefesh*, persons of a higher spiritual consciousness and, in that connection, he mentioned the importance of connection between such persons and the rest of the population, the *ba'alei ḥomer*, more materially-oriented people.[2] In that sense, he did not define the *kohanim* in a way relating to the sacrificial cult or as descendants of a particular family-line, but rather implied a parallel with the phenomenon of the Hasidic holy men of his own time in terms of their relationship with their followers. And Menahem Nahum of Chernobyl interpreted the words *b'nei Aharon*, "the descendants of Aaron" not as the actual descendants of Aaron, but rather as those who, in a very different sense, are Aaron's disciples as indicated in the familiar statement of Hillel in *Mishna Abot*, (I, 12), "Be as the students of Aaron, loving peace and pursuing peace, loving humankind and bringing them near to the Torah."[3]

Dov Baer of Mezhirech, in *Or Torah*, explains the *kohanim* as *mokhihim*, preachers who voice criticism, doing so however without any sense of self-exultation, a definition that might also relate to the role associated with the Hasidic *tzaddik* or holy man.[4] Elsewhere, the word *kohen* applies to a righteous person[5] or a com-

---

1. *Tol'dot Ya'akov Yosef* (*Tzav*), I, 294–95.

2. Ibid., I, 279–80 (*Tzav*) on Lev 6:2; also (*Emor*), I, 381.

3. *Ma'or 'einayim* (*Emor*), 47b–48a; *m. Abot*, 1.12.

4. *Or Torah* (*Emor*), 24b.

5. *No'am Elimelkh* (*Tzav*), 201, on Lev 6:3.

pletely righteous person.[6] In addition, both Elimelekh of Lyzhansk and Menahem Nahum of Chernobyl explained the term *kohen* both as one who serves God and also for God Himself insofar as God brings a person to inner healing, a function that they associated with the *kohanim*.[7]

As strange as it might appear, the homilists generally avoided any understanding of the priestly class as a status and role passed down through heredity from father to son and, instead, defined the *kohen* (priest) as one who serves God truthfully with inner integrity. An exception occurs in *No'am Elimelekh* where mention of that crucial genealogical detail that the *kohen* is the son of a *kohen* is accompanied with a strong warning that such privilege in terms of one's ancestry and pedigree includes within it the danger of haughtiness, and recommended that they should, in fact, erase such knowledge of their *yiḥus* (high pedigree) from their consciousness.[8] And Yitzhak Levi of Berditchev suggested that the Torah referred to them as *b'nai Aharon* (the sons of Aaron) precisely as a way to avoid any feeling of haughtiness on the part of the priests, reminding them that they were singled out "not due to any merit on their part, but rather due to that of Aaron."[9]

In the Torah, the *kohanim* guard the camp and the Tabernacle from all impurity (*tum'ah*). Such a state of *tum'ah* is identified with various skin-afflictions discussed in the portions *M'tzora'* and *Tzara'at*, where the *kohen* serves as a kind of medical examiner. He determined whether the person must leave the camp until the person recovers from that kind of physical affliction, whether the person's dwelling-place is afflicted and must hence be torn down, and when the afflicted person recovers to the point that the person can be allowed to return to the camp. The *kohen* in those chapters (Lev 12–15) does not treat the afflicted person but simply isolates him or her when necessary.

6. Ibid., (*Tazri'a*), 207 on Lev 13:2.

7. Ibid., (*M'tzora*), 210 on Lev 14:2; also 212; *Me'or 'einayim* (*M'tzora*), 44b and (*Emor*), 47b–48a.

8. Ibid., (*Emor*), 226–27.

9. *K'dushat Levi* (*Emor*), 200.

In the Hasidic homily-texts, the role of the *kohen* is understood very differently. He is neither a medical examiner nor one who physically isolates persons. His concern and relationship to the afflicted person is to ascertain the person's deeper moral or spiritual failing which brought on the physical impurity; that failing might be boastful speech or a haughty heart or lack of a soul-felt observance of the *mitzvot* (commandments). Furthermore, the *kohen* has the capacity to bring the person to a state of regret for his negative qualities.[10] This re-definition of the role of the biblical priest is one with which the homilist could identify in terms of how he grasped his role as the central figure of a Hasidic community. At times, the symptoms of a skin-affliction mentioned in the Torah-text are understood as the first signs of incomplete inner promptings of repentance, one which the *tzaddik* can then encourage in a way to lead to a healing of the self and one's spirit.[11] His concern is not with the symptoms of a skin-affliction but rather with a healing of the person's very self and character. And extending further, the afflictions come to be read more and more metaphorically, not as actual external bodily phenomena but rather as language symbolizing a person's inner failings and traits of character.[12]

ON LAWS OF SACRIFICE

Some Hasidic texts[13] echo the understanding expressed in the Zohar[14] that a sacrifice in which the physical animal is turned into smoke is part of a re-spiritualization of existence as physical existence itself is transformed into a more spiritual, sublime, and

---

10. *No'am Elimelekh* (*Tazri'a*), 207 on Lev 13:2; also *Or haMe'ir* (*M'tzora*), I, 314–15.

11. See *No'am Elimelekh*, (*Tazri'a*), 207 on Lev 13:49; also 212.

12. See *Ma'or vashemesh* on *Sh'mini* (III, 3b–4b), *Tazri'a* (III, 6a–7a), and *M'tzora* (III, 8ab.) And Wineman, *Letters of Light*, 152.

13. For example, *Maggid d'varav l'Ya'akov*, #190, 294–95 and #191, 295; *Divrat Sh'lomo* (*Vayikra*), III, 7.

14. Zohar I, 51ab, 65a, 176b–177a and III, 4b–5a, 35b. Also Tishby, *Mishnat haZohar*, II, 198–201.

unified reality. It transforms *yesh* (physical reality) into the original *ayin* (the Divine Oneness transcending physical reality), and restores contact and oneness with the infinite *Ein Sof*. But much more commonly in the homilies, the sacrifice itself, along with the altar and cultic ritual are read not in terms of having that kind of cosmic effect, but are understood instead as metaphors.

The first printed Hasidic book, *Tol'dot Ya'akov Yosef*, related to the practice of sacrificial offerings in light of what Ya'akov Yosef of Polonnoye considered a basic principle in understanding the Torah, namely that every one of the six-hundred-thirteen *mitzvot* (religious commands or prohibitions) must by nature be applicable to every person and every time. If at any time the act would not be applicable or possible—such as the long period of time when there is no Temple or possibility of performing sacrificial offerings—it would follow that the truer meaning of the commandment cannot be equated with its literal meaning.[15]

In the spirit of that principle of interpretation, Ya'akov Yosef of Polonnoye explained the words, *min hab'hemah* (from the animal) as *shel hab'hemi'ut adam*, a sacrifice of the animality of the person. And in the same location, the premier Hasidic homilist explained the sacrifice specified in the Torah as *t'filah* (prayer).[16] In the same vein, Ze'ev Wolf of Zhitomir rather surprisingly referred to the biblical *kohanim* as having taught "the ways of true prayer,"[17] a perfect example of one's describing figures from the distant past as an image of one's own temperament and mindset.

Much more commonly however in Hasidic homily-texts, the sacrifice is understood as symbolic not of prayer but rather of Torah-study, *talmud-torah*.

The word for burnt offering, *'olah*, relates to the verb-root meaning "to ascend, *la'alot*," presumably because in the course of burning on the altar the smoke ascends to a higher place in the atmosphere. On that basis Elimelekh of Lyzhansk explained the words, *Zot torat ha'olah* ("This is the law concerning the

---

15. *Tol'dot Ya'akov Yosef (Emor)*, I, 378, 4th homily.
16. Ibid., I, 268–69 (*Vayikra*), 2nd homily.
17. *Or haMe'ir (M'tzora')*, I, 315.

burnt-offering," Lev 6:2) as Torah-study itself ascending before God, and as a person's engaging in Torah-learning for its own sake having the power to ascend to serve as the means of atonement, hence fulfilling the role of the altar.[18] Echoing certain statements from the Talmud and the Zohar, Kalonymus Kalman Epstein of Krakow read the words, *Zot torat ha'olah* ("This is the law—*torah*—concerning the burnt offering," Lev 1: 2), as indicating that since God gave us the Torah, one needs neither a burnt offering nor a grain-offering, for (study of) Torah takes the place of everything to atone for all our iniquities."[19]

Furthermore, in his reading the phrase *'ol ha-mizbe'aḥ* ("*upon* the altar," Lev 6:2) as "*above* the altar," Elimelekh taught that Torah-study marked by the relevant mindset is "above the altar" in the sense of having greater effect than had the altar. A sacrificial offering on the altar, he explained, would atone for a single deed, while Torah-study conducted in a serious vein has the power to atone for all of one's misdeeds. And the earlier Yehiel Mikhel of Zlotchev, a peer of the *Besht* (the *Ba'al Shem Tov*), explained the very word *mizbe'aḥ* (altar) not literally but rather as *zove'aḥ yitzro*, as a person's slaughtering his own Evil Inclination.[20]

Elimelekh of Lyzhansk also read the words, *V'eish ha-mizbe'aḥ tukad bo* ("And fire of the alter will burn in it," Lev 6:2) metaphorically, as referring to an inner awakening and fiery passion (*hitlahavut*) kindled in the righteous person.[21] Menahem Nahum of Chernobyl similarly interpreted the *'olah* not as a burnt-offering as such, but rather in more abstract terms as "the *elevation*, the ascent of darkness to be transformed into light within a person, an event exemplifying the light hidden in the Torah, a light above the Letters which is not garbed in its coverings."[22]

Elimelekh understood various aspects of the laws concerning sacrifices symbolically. For example, he read the reference to the

18. *No'am Elimelekh* (*Tzav*), 199.

19. *Ma'or va-shemesh Ḥukkat*), part 4, 18b–19a. Note also Zohar III, 35a.

20. *Mayyim rabbim* (*B'shalaḥ*), 85.

21. *No'am Elimelekh* (*Tzav*), 200.

22. *Ma'or 'einayim* (*Tzav*), 43b.

linen garments of the priests that are to be removed and changed at a certain point (Lev 6:3) as the need on the part of the priest to make the effort to exchange an evil quality he has for a quality of the very opposite character. A *kohen* having a trait of anger, for example, is to make the effort to become merciful in every respect and hence to acquire a change of heart. And similarly, one who detects in his own makeup a trait of pride is called upon to intentionally lower himself in his own eyes, and one who is stingy must make the effort to become generous.[23]

He read similarly the verse that follows (Lev 6:4), requiring the *kohen* who removes the ashes from the altar to remove also his clothing and clad other clothes as indicating that a person cannot come to a higher level (of moral and spiritual behavior) until that person has unclad himself of all negative qualities. And he read the words which follow in the same verse, "And he shall remove the ashes beyond the camp," as indicating that a person's traits which may have been part of him since birth should not recur, but rather should be impacted by holiness. Later in the same section, it is written that an earthen vessel which has come in contact with levitical impurity should be broken and then rinsed with water (Lev 6:21), a verse which Elimelekh read as a person's shattering the defects in his own behavior, while the water refers "to Torah-study which is (traditionally) likened to water."[24]

A LARGER CONTEXT OF READING SUCH LAWS METAPHORICALLY

While the above Hasidic homilists read the altar and the sacrificial system symbolically, none of their comments reflect Maimonides' cultural or historical rationale suggesting that in light of the widespread prevalence of sacrifice at the time of the giving of the Torah, the Israelites would have been unable to grasp a way of worship

23. *No'am Elimelekh* (*Tzav*), 199.

24. Ibid., (*Tzav*), 201.

without sacrifice.[25] Nor do they voice a concern against the taking of animal life in the sacrificial process. Nor, with the exception of the clear position of Yitzhak of Radvil, does one meet with the explicit claim that, only due to their limited spiritual understanding following the making of the Golden Calf did the Israelites grasp the Torah in a way to mandate sacrifices.[26]

Instead, the details in that section of the Torah ordaining the system of sacrifices are read as elements that, like the section as a whole, must be decoded in a manner akin to rabbinic midrash. No direct negation of sacrifices as such is voiced in these readings, but the homilists read the cultic acts found in the Torah as a language for a purification of a person's behavior and attitudes through the study of Torah with personal, spiritual integrity. Hence, they generally read the biblical institution of sacrifice as a metaphor for the life of Torah-study and its program for the hallowing of life.

Occasionally, the same texts, in passing, mention, with a much more conventional ring, that due to our sins, we can no longer offer sacrifices as we once did, along with the hope that the Temple-cult will someday be re-instituted. But the highly creative interpretative energy sounded repeatedly in their symbolic reading of the verses and chapters of the Torah dealing with the cult point in a very different direction.

The two collections of the comments of Avraham Yehoshua Heschel of Apt (d. 1825) are insightful concerning the position of various Hasidic homilists who deeply questioned the practice of sacrifices even as they confronted the fact that the laws of sacrifice appear in the Torah itself and are hence viewed as Divinely revealed. Both collections appeared in print some decades after the death of the Apter *rebbe*, and both relate to the detailthat the opening word in the third book of the Torah (Lev 1:1), the word *Vayikra*, is written with a small letter-*aleph*.

Already in *Torat emet*, the earlier of the two compilations of the Apter master's commentary, the reduced size of that letter is

25. *Moreh n'vukhim*, part 3, ch. 21.

26. *Or Yitzḥak*, 210–11. See Wineman, "Hewn in the Divine Quarry," 198–99.

explained as alluding to the lower level of understanding on the part of the Israelites at that early time. In addition, that commentary claimed that the body of laws that follow that small *aleph* have their source in the earthly Tent of Meeting, which constituted, in effect, a lower spiritual space.[27] The second collection, *Oheiv Yisrael*, which appeared almost a decade later, similarly indicated that the laws of sacrifice which follow that small letter-*aleph* in the Torah-scroll are not on a par with other parts of the Torah which were revealed from a significantly higher, more sublime spiritual space.[28]

Both texts suggest an analysis of the syntax of that opening verse in Leviticus as pointing in two directions, addressing both the individual, capable of an ongoing depth of devotion and a more constant spiritual life, and also the larger population less capable of an ongoing attachment to God, with the implication that the sacrificial laws were given as a more external path and concession to the latter. In the eyes of the *Apter rebbe*, the sacrificial practices comprise a concession to the more human norm of those unable to grasp a more serious way of serving God, one having the potential of bringing blessing to all the worlds.[29]

In connection with the building of the Tabernacle (Exod 25–27), the same *Apter rebbe* suggested that each person contributed to that project along the lines of what that person valued most. Those who valued gold, silver and copper above all else gave such metals for the building of the Tabernacle (*Mishkan*), and God not only praised their intention but even accommodated the Divine presence to the dimensions of the *Mishkan*, while those who valued most what is spiritual in character understood the meaning of the Tabernacle as each person's making one's very life and self and even the limbs of one's body a dwelling-place for the Divine.[30]

27. *Torat emet* (*Vayikra*), 22b. Also *Or haHayyim*, II, 1a–2b in reference to Lev 1:1.

28. *Oheiv Yisrael* (*Vayikra*), 59b; note also (*Pinḥas*), 75b.

29. *Torat emet* (*Vayikra*), 23a.

30. *Oheiv Yisrael* (*T'rumah*), 47a-48a. See Wineman, "Sufis in the Hasidic *Mishkan*."

Beyond the implications of the rationale based on a detail in the way that one letter is written in reduced size in the Torah-scroll, the direction of much of the Hasidic homily-literature touching on this issue expresses the vast distance which the Hasidic teachers intuitively felt to separate the practices of the biblical priestly sacrificial cult from the ethos of *p'nimi'ut,* innerness, so central to Hasidic piety.

9

Moses—Between Person and Metaphor[1]

In many passages in the Hasidic homily-texts, Moses is depicted as "the faithful shepherd," *ha-ro'eh ha-ne'eman,* and in those examples as in many similar references to Moses, the Hasidic homily-texts relate to Moses very much as a person, a singular personality with a particular life-span, as he appears in the Torah itself. Moses is viewed as a human agent and messenger of Divine Revelation. This is the case even when the details of the biblical account of his life are often interpreted in a way to reflect rather specific Hasidic themes and when Moses is presented as an intimation or prototype of the *tzaddik*, the Hasidic holy man. One also notes, however, various other passages in the same literature that refer to him in a much more abstract manner. In such passages Moses appears less as a person as such than as a symbolic figure or metaphor and as one who, in some significant sense, transcends his life-span and his own hour of time as found in the Torah.

---

1. This chapter appeared in *Hebrew Studies*, Vol. LIX, 2018, 209–219.

AN INTRINSIC RELATIONSHIP BETWEEN MOSES, HIS PEOPLE, AND THE TORAH

In *Degel maḥaneh Efrayim*, for example, Moses is not simply the head and leader of the entire Israelite population of his time, but the text speaks of all the Israelites as being sparks and portions of Moses himself as he, in some real sense, "included all of them." The latter concept, found already in Lurianic texts,[2] echoes rabbinic sources which speak of the soul of Adam as encompassing all souls—or, at least the souls of the Israelites.[3] In the *Degel*, Moses' entire generation consists of sparks of their leader who is referred to as their father and as being equivalent, in some sense, to the totality of the members of that generation. Furthermore, the claim is expressed that it was precisely because all those who comprised the entire population were, in their very essence, sparks of Moses that he was able to raise them up to a higher level.[4] Although this conception has older roots, it is not difficult to read this idea in relation to the conception of the leader and center of a Hasidic community, a role that was still in its period of emergence during the lifetime of Moshe Hayyim Efrayim of Sedilikov, a grandson of the Ba'al Shem Tov.

Elsewhere, the same text explains the words which occur in the Torah in connection with Moses' mother, Yocheved, *v'teire oto ki tov hu*, ("And she saw that he was good," Exod 2:2), in that the word *tov* (good) necessarily refers to the Torah. Hence Moses and the Torah are, in that sense, one, with the claim that also Jethro understood "that Moses is truly and actually the Torah."[5] The same text clearly identifies Moses as a personification of Torah, hence going beyond his biblical role as the agent of Revelation or God's messenger to the people to indicate that his very being is, as it were, one with the Torah which he intrinsically and personally

---

2. Hayyim Vital, *Sha'ar haGilgulim*, Intro., #34, p. 97, n. 1. Note Fine, *Physics of the Soul*, 314, n. 35.

3. *Midr. Exod.*, 40:3 (*Ki Tissa*), and *Tanh.* (*Ki Tissa*), #12.

4. *Degel maḥaneh Efrayim* (Bo), 96; 109 (*Yitro*).

5. Ibid., (*Yitro*), 108.

embodied.[6] That view interestingly, recalls and perhaps echoes deeper roots in the Hellenistic conception of the ideal king as "the embodiment of law," a conception already expressed in connection with Moses in the writings of Philo.[7]

An expression of this identification of Moses with the Torah is clearly spelled out in a passage in *Degel maḥaneh Efrayim* with the claim that Moses was the secret (*sod*) of the Torah, and that "everything God created was for Moses, as he truly and actually is the Torah."[8] This concept is given a broader context in that the *Degel* also refers to Abraham in a similar way, "for Abraham really is the Torah as all the Torah was included in him."[9] The force of such a statement views the Torah not only as a document but also as the very essence and being of a person who is its embodiment. The same text suggests that words from Ps 97:11, *Or zaru'a la-tzaddik*, "Light is sown for the righteous one" refer to Moses who was the very light of the entire Torah, and for this reason, the Torah in its entirety was revealed through him.[10]

That same homiletical work explains Moses' intrinsic relationship with the Torah also in that he was the "husband of the Torah." That concept echoes readings of the wording of Deut 33:1, *Moshe ish ha'elohim* ("Moses, a man of God"), which came to be interpreted as the husband or bridegroom of the *Shekhinah* (the Divine Presence), and also the wording from Num 7:1 where the word *kalot* ("when he completed" in reference to the building of the Tabernacle) was read as an intimation of the word *kalah* ("bride").[11] On the basis of that wording and its association, Efrayim of Sedilikov proceeded further to broaden that image to apply to any person in any generation who studies Torah *lishmah* (for its own sake rather than for any personal advantage). Such a person

---

6. Ibid., (*Yitro*), 109.

7. Meeks, *The Prophet-King*, 191; also Goodenough, *An Introduction to Philo Judaeus*, 38–39.

8. *Degel maḥaneh Efrayim* (*Yitro*), 108.

9. Ibid., (*Lekh-l'kha*) 13; (*Vayera*) 23–24, and (*Ḥayye Sarah*), 29–30.

10. Ibid., (*Va'etḥanan*), 230.

11. Ibid., (*Yitro*), 108, based on Zohar III, 148a.

represents and assumes the quality of Moses and similarly becomes a bridegroom of the Torah, and hence the secrets or mysteries of the Torah are revealed to him insofar as "a woman discloses her secrets only to her husband."[12]

Not only does Moses encompass within himself the entirety of his particular generation, but his soul or consciousness recurs potentially throughout all generations. These comments represent a definite level of abstraction as they refer to Moses less as an individual person than as an embodiment of his people as a whole and of their basic Scripture. The *Degel*, interestingly, maintained that "Rabbi Shimon bar Yohai (who was traditionally regarded as the author of the Zohar) represented the aspect of Moses and, proceeding further, that "in every generation there is one who shares the aspect of Moses" in deriving, through interpretation, the meaning of the Torah of Moses.[13]

With this understanding, the sense of Moses' utter uniqueness through all of time is transformed into Moses' serving as a metaphor that alludes also to others through the generations who participate in the pursuit of Torah-study with a purity of motivation. This expansion of Moses' ultimate identity beyond his individual existence illumines a comment which we have already met, in the same text, concerning the small size of that letter *aleph* as it appears in the opening word of the third book of the Torah (Lev 1:1): "Although Moses received the Torah (at Sinai), he himself understood it only limitedly, but in the future God will bring us to a much improved understanding at which time that small letter will become large!"[14]

In context, others in later generations are not only able to clarify and understand the truer, deeper meaning of what was revealed to Moses, but in doing so they assume something of the personhood of Moses himself. This tendency received special emphasis in the comments of Efrayim of Sedilikov, likely expressing

12. Ibid., based on Zohar II, 99b.
13. Ibid., (*Sh'mini*), 164.
14. Ibid., (*Vayikra*), 149.

an implied identification of the role of the leaders (*tzaddikim*) of the emerging Hasidic communities with that of the biblical Moses.

In a parallel direction, one encounters in some Hasidic homily-texts the idea that Moses' soul will ultimately return as the messianic redeemer. The very first deliverer, in that sense, will also be the final redeemer, an idea found already in midrashic sources,[15] and an identification significant in the way both an earlier figure, Moses Hayyim Luzzatto,[16] and also Rebbe Nahman of Bratzlav[17] understood their own role and truer identity. Further deepening that connection, Aharon ben Asher of Karlin connected the words, *ki tov hu*, "that he (the infant, Moses) is good" (Exod 2:2), with mention of the Tree of Knowledge of Good and Evil in the Garden of Eden, *ki tov ha'etz l'ma'akhal* ("that the tree is good for eating," Gen 3:6), identifying Moses as the one who will ultimately annul the impact of that primordial sin of the First Man.[18]

MOSES' RECURRENT EXISTENCE

Elimelekh of Lyzhansk viewed Moses as the most perfect example of the *tzaddik*, literally, "the righteous person," though the term came to signify more precisely a holy man and, with rise of Hasidism, a leader and center of any of the emerging Hasidic communities. As a result of the *tzaddik*'s own inner awakening, God causes holy influx (*shefa'*) to descend from above into the inner being of the *tzaddik*, influx which then awakens people's hearts to serve God in a state of true awakening and response.[19] The intent of Elimelekh—it would appear—was not to view the *tzaddikim* as being on a par with Moses, but rather to view Moses as a representative par excellence of the later class of Hasidic teachers and leaders.

15. *Sipre*, #355, 147b on Deut 33:21 (*V'zot hab'rakha*), also *Midr. Exod.* (*Sh'mot*), 2.4, and *Midr. Num.* (*Ḥukkat*), 10:13.

16. Tishby, *Messianic Mysticism*, 198.

17. Green, *Tormented Master*, 119.

18. *Beit Aharon*, 55b on Exod 2:2.

19. *No'am Elimelekh* (*Yitro*), 148–49.

Repeatedly, Elimelekh referred to "the *tzaddik* who was called by the name, *Moshe* (Moses),"[20] who was able, in his state of *d'veikut*, deep inner attachment to the Divine, to ascend to the higher worlds where he had the capacity to "sweeten the judgments," transforming punitive actions into Divine compassion. That function came to be considered basic to the role of the *tzaddik*.[21] Elimelekh also viewed Moses as one who was in perpetual doubt concerning his worthiness to fulfill that role[22] reflecting the view, voiced in his collection of homiletical notes, *No'am Elimilekh*, that the true *tzaddik* is, paradoxically, one who does not see himself as such.[23]

The reader recalls that the text in *No'am Elimelekh* furthermore voices that interesting conception that Moses had to die in the wilderness leaving his work incomplete, "so that in every generation he might return and re-appear in the souls of *tzaddikim* who, like him, would be able to 'sweeten the judgments.'"[24] We recall the idea that Moses had to die before being able to enter the Land not due to any fault or failure on his part, but rather because only through death would he be able to fulfill, over many generations, his more complete role and promise. While the idea that the soul of Moses extends and appears through all the generations can be noted already in the Jerusalem Talmud[25] and is found in Lurianic sources,[26] it probably received its clearest expression in *No'am Elimelekh*, a homily-text which served largely as a significant statement of the role of the Hasidic holy man.

20. Ibid., (*B'shalaḥ*), 141–42 and (*T'rumah*), 153.

21. Ibid., (*Yitro*), 153–54.

22. Ibid., (*Sh'mot*), 119.

23. Ibid., (*No'aḥ*), 23–24; also (*Sh'mot*) 121 and (*T'rumah*) 174.

24. Ibid., (*D'varim*), 315; also (*T'tzaveh*), 185.

25. *j. Sanh* 4.2. See Giller, *The Enlightened Will Shine*, 146, n. 119.

26. Hayyim Vital, *Sha'ar hagilgulim*, Intro. #20, 54. Note Fine, *Physics of the Soul*, 315, n. 36.

MOSES AS *DA'AT*

Hasidism inherited from kabbalistic tradition the identification of certain key biblical personages with the *s'firot*, the emanations of the Divine in its infinite state which underlie all of being. While in the Zohar, Moses is most often associated with the *s'firah Netzaḥ* (triumph or eternity), in some sources he is identified with *Tiferet* (*Raḥamim*) conveying the sense of the Written Torah which is copied from the Primordial Torah.[27] In Hasidic teaching, evident already in *Tol'dot Ya'akov Yosef*,[28] he came to be associated with *Da'at* (literally "knowledge"), which is itself an amalgam of the *s'firot Ḥokhmah* (wisdom) and *Binah* (understanding). *Da'at* came to be attached to the pattern of the *s'firot* already in the late thirteenth century.[29] This realignment of his role might perhaps echo the talmudic motif that Moses had been given the key to forty-nine of the fifty paths of understanding, and according to the pertinent rabbinical sources Moses was not given the fiftieth key simply because "You have made him a little lower than Divine" (Ps 8:6).[30] Of all the *s'firot*, *Da'at* most clearly speaks to what is central to Hasidic teaching: a consciousness rooted in a person's very innerness and one's living with the understanding that God is the innerness of all being and is, on a deeper, more ultimate level, the sole reality. Identifying a person with a *s'firah* had the effect of making that individual less a person than a metaphor.

T'MIDI'UT: MOSES, LIKE THE TORAH AS A WHOLE, TRANSCENDS TIME

With the premise that all commandments found in the Torah must be applicable in all times, in the very first printed Hasidic text, *Tol'dot Ya'akov Yosef*, Ya'akov Yosef of Polonnoye posed a question

27. Idel, *Absorbing Perfections*, 458.

28. *Tol'dot Ya'akov Yosef* (*Sh'mini*), I, 296b.

29. Scholem, *Kabbalah*, 107.

30. *b. Rosh.* 21b and *b. Ned.* 38a, also *b. Erub.* 13b. See Ginzberg, *Legends*, VI, 284, n. 25 and Idel, *Absorbing Perfections*, 209 and 551, n. 62.

concerning how certain commands, seemingly bearing an intrinsic relationship to specific situations and points-in-time, can be applied and fulfilled in later generations.[31] He also proceeded to interpret, often by the use of parables and allegorical readings, various episodes and details of the toraitic narrative in a way to define a much more inner meaning of the narrative, one that is, by nature, not time-bound. For example—as we have seen—drawing from his own rather ascetic mindset he explained that *Mitzrayim* (Egypt) connotes, on a deeper level, life in this world and its delights, which are naturally subject to *meitzarim* (narrow straits and limitations including death itself).[32] He defined the Exodus from Egypt—as we've read—allegorically as the departure from impurity to holiness,[33] and understood Pharaoh as representing the qualities both of stubbornness—which can hence apply also to any stubborn Israelite[34]—and of *shikh'ha* (forgetting),[35] whereas Moses represents *Da'at*, the polar opposite of forgetting.[36]

In *Or ha-me'ir*, Ze'ev Wolf of Zhitomir (d. 1800) defined that principle or method of interpretation as *t'midi'ut* (from the word *tamid*, "always"), the recognition that everything in the Torah necessarily refers to all of time, past, present and future. That very principle, in fact, became primary in Ze'ev Wolf's understanding of the Torah-text. As the Torah preceded Creation, its very Letters are rooted in eternity, and consequently the meaning of any narrative applies not only to some point in the past but, on a deeper level, to all of time.[37]

Regarding such narratives as accounts of the past limits and even negates their larger import. For example, the Zhitomir preacher understood God's command to Noah to take with him all kinds of food not only for Noah's family but also for the animals

---

31. *Tol'dot Ya'akov Yosef* (*Vayehi*), I, 123–24 and (*Bo*), I, 146.

32. Ibid., I, 136 (*Sh'mot*, #6) and 148 (*Bo*, #5).

33. Ibid., I, 144 (*Ve'era*, #2) and 174 (*Bo*, #1).

34. Ibid., I, 146 (*Bo*, #2).

35. Ibid., I, 175 (*B'shalah*, #6).

36. Ibid., I, 196 (*Sh'mini*, #6).

37. *Or haMe'ir* I (*Yitro*), 144–45.

(Gen 6:19–22) as affirming, for all, a connection with the entire range of created things and an understanding that the various forms of non-human life as well as plant life and even inert nature were all created with wisdom in a way to awaken one's heart to God.[38] And he understood the episode of the Burning Bush in the desert (Exod 3:1–10) as a repeated call, in the form of some lack or disturbing occurrence, to each person in every generation who can then turn to engage in selfless prayer with the intent of repairing the higher spheres.[39]

Even more emphatically and consistently than Ya'akov Yosef of Polonnoye, Ze'ev Wolf sought to define, in connection with all elements in the toraitic narrative, a core, spiritual principle that can apply to all of time, lifting what appears as a one-time occurrence to what recurs in all generations and, in the process, defining the happening in a much more abstract way. In this sense, *Or ha-me'ir* clearly exemplifies the tendency that Gershom Scholem referred to as mysticism's "aloofness to history" with its focus, instead, upon the devotee's inner life in the present moment.[40] To the mind of Ze'ev Wolf of Zhitomir, the account of bondage in Egypt occurs throughout the course of time in every person's servitude to forces and impulses within the self. Similarly, the deliverance from Egyptian bondage occurs in any person's life with the realization that the higher Wisdom is concealed and clothed within all existence and, hence, with that person's attunement to the sublime dimension within all that is.[41] Ze'ev Wolf translated that core mindset, implied perhaps in numerous other Hasidic homily-texts, into a basic principle of interpretation.

According to Ze'ev Wolf, "Even if subjugation and exile in Egypt had never occurred, the commandments and the festivals which Moses spoke to Israel would not be voided, as they relate not to the 'lower' physical Departure from Egypt but rather, on a more abstract level, to the 'higher' (and recurrent) spiritual Departure

38. Ibid., (*No'aḥ*), I, 11.
39. Ibid., (*Sh'mot*), I, 107–9.
40. Scholem, *Major Trends*, 19.
41. *Or haMe'ir* (*Vayera*), I, 27.

from Egypt"[42]—though there was also need for the physical (earthly) Exodus to occur in order that people might grasp that higher (spiritual) Exodus[43] which is experienced by every person at all times.[44] Clad in the lower, more concrete Pharaoh in the account of the Exodus is a higher Pharaoh, a persistent tendency opposing the aspect of *Da'at* throughout time[45] as one's truer self becomes lost in the pursuit of material concerns. "Every Israelite has his own Pharaoh who confronts him,"[46] robbing him of his moral and spiritual compass.[47]

The conception of Moses' recurrent presence through all the generations as a manifestation of *Da'at*, is, for Ze'ev Wolf, the very basic and prime example of *t'midi'ut*. "Just as we find the expanded presence of Moses in every single generation," so also Esau and Balaam and Balak and Korah recur through time in every generation.[48] Moses transcends his mortal life-span and his one-time existence as a biblical figure to serve as a metaphor of a spiritual consciousness which extends throughout all the generations. Ze'ev Wolf of Zhitomir brought a proof text in the words, *mah she-hayah hu she-yihyeh* ("What was will be," Eccl 1:9), as together the first letter of the first three words spell the name, *Moshe* (Moses)![49] Furthermore, Moses is present within each person who has any degree of spiritual understanding and sensitivity. Hence, "every person who has within him *da'at kono* (a spiritual awareness of his Master), is called Moses.[50]

The association of Moses with the *s'firah*, *Da'at*, the conception of Moses as recurrent in all generations and Hasidism's primary ethos of *p'nimi'ut* (innerness) all contributed to this

42. Ibid., (*D'rush l'Pesaḥ*), I, 229–30.

43. Ibid., I, 233,

44. Ibid., (*Sh'mot*), I, 113.

45. Ibid., (*Bo*), I, 126.

46. Ibid., (*B'shalaḥ*), I, 132.

47. Ibid., I, 135.

48. Ibid., (*Yitro*), I, 145.

49. Ibid., (*Koraḥ*), II, 101.

50. Ibid., (*Yitro*), I, 151 and (*Ki Tissa*), 193.

conception of Moses as the ongoing spiritual quality within human consciousness.

THE BURIAL OF MOSES

Menahem Nahum of Chernobyl interpreted the verse relating to Moses' burial-site ("And to this very day no person knows his burial place," Deut 34:6) to suggest that though *Da'at*, identified with Moses, was hidden in the Torah, it is nevertheless available to every person who studies the Torah according to the full extent of his intelligence. And in that sense, according to Menahem Nahum, the seventh day of the month, *Adar*, the traditional date of the death of Moses, is also Moses' birth-date, as with his death, Moses nevertheless assumes renewed existence in every generation.[51]

Ze'ev Wolf of Zhitomir would very likely have agreed with that thought, even as he interpreted the episode of the burial of Moses (Deut 34:6) as indicating that Moses was buried in stories (*sippurim*). That formulation echoes an earlier claim, sounded in the latter strata of the Zoharic literature, *Ra'ya m'heimna* and *Tikkunei Zohar*, that Moses was buried in the Mishna—meaning that the *Da'at* conveyed in the Torah itself was "buried," in a metaphorical sense, by those preoccupied solely with its legal dimension while by-passing what critics viewed as its more centrally significant and more sublime mystic interpretation. The intent of such criticism was not antinomian in character but, rather, protested an exclusive emphasis upon the legal interpretation of the Torah to the point of endless, complex legal discourse and argumentation which was thought to obscure the higher level of consciousness present in the Torah. In the words of that accusation, the exclusive legal preoccupation served (to bring to its death and) to bury the more essential aspect of the Torah and of Moses, identified as *Da'at*.[52]

---

51. *Ma'or 'einayim* (*T'rumah*), 38a. An earlier explanation is noted in *Yalqut*, I, #965 (*Zot hab'rakhah*).

52. *Tikkunei Zohar*, I, 27b-28a; also II, 118a, and III, 17a. Note Giller, *The Enlightened Will Shine*, 60–75.

Ze'ev Wolf echoed that much earlier analogy for the purpose of a very different contention as he read the statement of Moses' burial as indicating that Moses, symbolizing *Da'at*, is buried in stories by those who grasp the Torah essentially in terms of its narrative-level to the detriment of the deeper spiritual meaning to which those very stories allude. That tendency, he maintained, serves in effect to bury *Da'at*, the deeper level of spiritual awareness and sensitivity, associated with Moses. With an exclusive or exaggerated focus on the Torah's narrative and its details—he wrote—the very letters comprising those tales remain dry and devoid of any real life.[53]

This polemic against an exaggerated attention to the Torah's narratives is, of course, not original with Ze'ev Wolf of Zhitomir. It is conveyed quite clearly in the Zohar itself which refers to the Torah as having a body and soul and also garments: the law comprises the body of the Torah; its soul is the deeper, mystic understanding of the Torah's content, while the stories serve merely as garments of the Torah. That passage in the Zohar goes on to liken the narratives in the Torah to a bottle which is necessary only so that it might hold the wine contained within it.[54] On a broader vista one meets with the kabbalistic view that the Torah originally consisted of letters with no separation between them, letters that signified no objective meaning open to human mental grasp but were open rather to purely experiential connection and were thought in their totality to signify the Name of God, while the separation of letters into words engendered the toraitic narrative, a materialization of what in itself is of an infinitely higher character.[55] One might suggest the analogy of experiencing a complex and profound musical composition compared with a deflating attempt to reduce the same work to the level of a scenario.

Stories appear in the Torah, Ze'ev Wolf contended, as a Divine concession to the Israelites who, otherwise, would simply have been unable to grasp the Torah. Unlike Moses himself who

---

53. *Or haMe'ir* (*Vayera*), I, 33.

54. Zohar III, 152a (*B'ha'alotkha*).

55. *Or haMe'ir* (*Korah*), II, 108; Idel, *Absorbing Perfections*, 369–85.

had no need for stories, the other Israelites could grasp the Torah only after it had undergone many contractions (*tzimtzumim*) and acquired many garments which comprised "the thickness of the cloud" ('*av he'anan*, Exod 19:9).[56] In contrast, the intelligent person must unclad the Torah of its garment of materiality and clad it, instead, in a spiritual form.[57]

Ze'ev Wolf, in his own way, read the Torah's story-elements not as significant in themselves but rather as allusions to what he viewed as the Torah's deeper level and as metaphors of what occurs repeatedly over time. To his mind, even the episode of Moses' burial is such a story which has to be unpacked to understand the story's deeper truth which transcends any particular point in time or space.

56. Ibid., (*Yitro*), I, 151.
57. Ibid., (*Ki Tissa*), I, 194.

Moses was equal to all Israel,
and each person of Israel needs to have
b'ḥinat Moshe (the aspect of
the quality and essence of Moses).
—*K'dushat Levi* (*Re'eh*), 261

In one respect, the concluding chapter of the Torah emphasizes the absolute singularity of Moses, "And there has never again risen a prophet in Israel like Moses" (Deut 34:10). And in a very contrasting respect, it is mentioned in *Tikkunei Zohar* (112a–114a) that the soul of Moses returns to the world in every generation in the form of the Righteous of that generation who represent, in their very being, the supernal Wisdom with which Moses was gifted. How can both these very contradictory positions be true? Moses himself, as an individual person, will not return, as it is written, "And you will not cross over (the river)" (Deut 34:4), but in God's perception of the world, a view that transcends time itself, past and future are the same. [Avraham Hayyim ben Gedaliah, *Oraḥ l'ḥayyim* (*Zot hab'rakhah*), 394–95, abridged].

Bibliography

TRADITIONAL AND HASIDIC TEXTS

'Avodat hakodesh (Meir Gabbai). B'nei Brak: S. Harari, 1995.

(Babylonian Talmud, BT) *Talmud Bavli*. 20 vols. Jerusalem: Telman, 1980–81. English translation: *The Babylonian Talmud*. Edited by Isadore Epstein. 18 vols. London: Soncino, 1978.

Beit Aharon (Aharon ben Asher). Brody: n.p., 1875.

Bei'ur 'ol haTorah (Bahya ben Asher). Warsaw: Natan ben Zvi Schriftgissen, 1853.

B'reshit rabba. J. Theodor-Ch. Albeck, *Berischit rabba: mit Kritischen Apparat und Kommentar*. Berlin: Akademie fur die Wissenschaft de Judentums, 1931.

Degel Maḥaneh Efrayim (Moshe Hayyim Efrayim of Sedelikov). Koretz: n.p., 1810. Reprint. Jerusalem: n.p., 1963.

Divrat Sh'lomo (Shlomo Lutsker). Zolkiew: n.p., 1848. Reprint. New Square, NY: Friedman, n.d.

Divre Moshe (Moshe ben Dan Shoham of Dolina). Polonnoye: n.p., 1801. Reprint. B'nai Brak, 2003.

Ḥamishah ḥumshe Torah im arba'im ush'monah perushim. 5 vols. Austria: Judischen verlag, n.d.

Ḥayyei Moharan (Nathan of Sternhartz). Jerusalem: Vardi, 1962.

Ḥesed l'Avraham (Avraham ha-Malakh, ben Dov Baer). Czernowitz: n.p., 1851. Reprint. Warsaw: n.p., 1899.

Ḥovot hal'vavot (Bahya ibn Pekudah). Translated by Yehuda Ibn Tibbin. Jerusalem: Eshkol, 1969.

K'dushat Levi (Levi Yitzhak of Berditchev). Slavuta: n.p., 1798; expanded version: n.p., 1811. Reprint. Jerusalem: Torat ha-netzah, 1993.

Kol simḥah (Simhah Bunam of Parshisha). Breslau: n.p., 1859. Reprint. Jerusalem: Nofet Tzofim, 1997.

Bibliography

Maggid d'varav leYa'akov (Dov Baer of Mezhirech). Edited by Rifka Schatz-Uffenheimer. Jerusalem: Magnus, 1976.

Ma'or 'einayim (Menahem Nahum of Chernobyl). Slavuta: n.p., 1798. Reprint. Jerusalem: n.p., 1984.

Ma'or vashemesh 'ol hamishah humshot Torah, (Kalonymus Kalman Epstein). Breslau, 1842. Reprint. Warsaw: B'nai Shmu'el Argelbrend, 1875–77. Translation of passages with commentary, A. Wineman, *Letters of Light.* Eugene, OR: Pickwick, 2015.

Mayyim Rabbim (Yehiel Mikhel of Zlozetch). Warsaw: n.p., 1899.

Midrash Rabbah. Warsaw: Levin-Epstein, 1924. 2 vols. English translation, 10 vols. Edited by Harry Freedman and Maurice Simon. London: Soncino, 1983.

Midrash Ekha rabbah. Edited by Solomon Buber. Vilna: Romm, 1908.

Midrash Tanna'im. Edited by David Hoffman. Berlin: n.p., 1908. Reprint. Tel-Aviv, 1962.

M'khilta de-Rabbi Yishma'el. Edited by Ish-shalom and Jacob Lauterbach. New York: OM, 1948.

Mishneh Torah (Moses Maimonides' Code of Jewish Law). 12 vols. Jerusalem: Hatzaat Shabse Frankel, 2000.

Moreh N'vukhim (Moses Maimonides). Jerusalem, Mosad ha-Rav Kook, 1981. *The Guide of the Perplexed*, translated by Michael Friedlander. New York: Hebrew Publishing, 1952; *The Guide of the Perplexed*, translated by Shlomo Pines. 2 vols. Chicago: University of Chicago Press, 1963.

No'am Elimelekh (Elimelekh of Lyzhansk). Lemberg: n.p., 1788. Reprint. Jerusalem: n.p., 1992.

Oheiv Yisra'el (Avraham Yehoshua Heschel of Apt). Zhitomir: n.p., 1863. Reprint. New York: n.p., 1956.

Orah l'hayyim, (Avraham Hayyim of Zlotshuv). Berditchev: n.p., 1817.

Or ha-hayyim (Hayyim ben Moshe Attar). 2 vols. Venice: n.p., 1742.

Or ha-me'ir (Ze'ev Wolf of Zhitomir). Koretz. n.p., 1798. Reprint. 2 vols. Ashdod: Blotnik, 1995.

Or Torah (Dov Ber of Mezhirech). Slavuta: n.p., n.d. Reprint. Lublin: n.p., 1910.

Or Yitzhak (Yitzhak of Radvil). Jerusalem, 1961. Reprint. Jerusalem: El he-harim, 1992.

Pirke d'Rabbi Eleazer with commentary of David Luria. Warsaw: Bomberg, 1852. Reprint. Jerusalem: n.p., 1963.

P'nine haHasidut. Jerusalem: *Makhon P'nine haHasidut*, 1980.

P'sikta d'Rav Kahana. Edited by Solomon Buber. Lyck: n.p., 1868. Edited by Bernard Mandelbaum. New York: Jewish Theological Seminary, 1962.

Sefer Shivhei haBesht. Edited by Sh. A. Horodezky. Tel Aviv: Dvir, 1947. English translation, *In Praise of the Baal Shem Tov*, translated by Dan Ben-Amos and Jerome R. Mintz. Bloomington, IN: Indiana University Press, 1970.

Sefer hat'filot kol ha-shanah, Authorized Daily Prayer Book, Rev. ed. Edited by Joseph Hertz. New York: Bloch, 1959.

Sefer ha-yashar. Venice: n.p., 1624. Reprint. Jerusalem: Mosad Bialik, 1986.

Sefer sippurei maʾasiyot. Jerusalem: Hasidei Braslav, 1968. English translation, *Nahman of Bratslav: The Tales*, translated by Arnold Band. New York: Paulist, 1978.

S'fat emet (Jerusalem: n.p.) Pietrkov, 1905–8. Select Passages translated with commentary by Arthur Green, *The Language of Truth*. Philadelphia: Jewish Publication Society, 2005.

Shaʾar haGilgulim (Hayyim Vital). Przemysl: n.p., 1875.

Sifre d'vei Rav. Edited by Ish-shalom. Vienna, n p., 1864; New York: OM, 1948.

Tiferet Uziʾel (Uziel ben Zvi). Warsaw: n.p., 1863.

Tikkunei ha-zohar. Edited by Reuven Margoliot. Tel Aviv: Mosad haRav Kook, 1978.

Tol'dot Yaʾakov Yosef (Yaʾakov Yosef of Polonnoye). Koretz: n.p., 1780. Reprint. 2 vols. Jerusalem: Agudat Beit Vi'alipali, 1973.

Torah Or (Shneur Zalman of Liady). Lemberg: n.p., 1851.

Torat emet (Avraham Yehoshua Heschel of Apt). Lemberg: n.p., 1854.

Yalkut Shimʾoni, 2 vols. Jerusalem: Bezalel Landau, 1960.

Zohar: Sefer haZohar, 3 vols. Jerusalem: Or haZohar, 1954. *Zohar*, Pritzker edition, translated by Daniel Chanan Matt. 9 vols. Stanford, CA: Stanford University Press, 2004–16.

MODERN STUDIES AND REFERENCE WORKS

The Authorized Daily Prayer Book. Edited by Joseph Hertz. New York: Bloch, 1948.

Betz, Hans Dichter, ed. *The Bible as a Document of the University*. Chico, CA: Scholars, 1981.

Buber, Martin. *Moses*. Oxford: East and West Library, 1947.

A Dictionary of Literary Terms and Literary Theory. Edited by John Anthony Cuddon and C. E. Preshen. Oxford: Blackwell, 1998.

A Dictionary of Modern Critical Terms. Edited by Roger Fowler. London: Routledge and Paul, 1988.

Eliade, Mircea. *Myths, Dreams, and Mysteries*. Translated by Philip Mairet. New York: Harper Torchbooks, 1967.

Fine, Lawrence. *Physician of the Soul, Healer of the Cosmos: Isaac Luria and His Kabbalistic Fellowship*. Stanford, CA: Stanford University Press, 2003.

Fishbane, Michael. *The Exegetical Imagination: On Jewish Thought and Theology*. Cambridge: Harvard University Press, 1998.

———. *The Garments of Torah: Essays in Biblical Hermeneutics*. Bloomington, IN: Indiana University Press, 1989.

Frankel, Viktor. *Man's Search for Meaning: An Introduction to Logotherapy*. Boston: Beacon, 1963.

Frazer, Sir James. *The Golden Bough: A Study in Magic and Religion*. 12 vols. London: Macmillan, 1911–36.

Giller, Pinchas. *The Enlightened Will Shine: Symbolization and Theurgy in the Later Strata of the Zohar.* Albany, NY: State University of New Year Press, 1993.

Ginzberg, Louis. *The Legends of the Jews.* 7 vols. Philadelphia: Jewish Publication Society, 1954.

Goodenough, Erwin R. *An Introduction to Philo Judaeus.* New Haven: Yale University Press, 1940.

Green, Arthur. *The Language of Truth.* Philadelphia: Jewish Publication Society, 1998.

———. *See My Face, Speak My Name: A Contemporary Jewish Theology.* Northvale, NJ; Aronson, 1992.

———. *Tormented Master: A Life of Rabbi Nahman of Bratslav.* Tuscaloosa, AL: The University of Alabama Press, 1979.

Handelman, Susan A. *The Slayers of Moses: The Emergence of Rabbinic Interpretation in Modern Literary Theory.* Albany, NY: State University of New York Press, 1982.

Haran, Menahem. *Temples and Temple-Service in Ancient Israel.* Oxford: Clarendon, 1978.

Heinemann, Yitzhak. *Darkhei ha-aggadah.* Jerusalem: Magnus, 1954.

Heschel, Abraham Joshua. *God in Search of Man: A Philosophy of Judaism.* Philadelphia, Jewish Publication Society, 1956.

Idel, Moshe. *Absorbing Perfections: Kabbalah and Interpretation.* New Haven: Yale University Press, 2002.

———. *Kabbalah: New Perspectives.* New Haven: Yale University Press, 2002.

Klawans, Jonathan. *Purity, Sacrifice and the Temple.* Oxford: Oxford University Press, 2006.

Magid, Shaul. *Hasidism on the Margin.* Madison, WI: The University of Wisconsin Press, 2003.

Margolin, Ron. *Mikdash adam: hahafnamah hadatit ve'itzum ḥayyei hadat hap'nimiyim b'reshit haḥasidut.* Jerusalem: Magnes, 2005.

Meeks, Wayne. *The Prophet-King: Moses Traditions and the Johannine Christology.* Leiden: Brill, 1967.

Midrash Unbound: Transformations and Innovations. Edited by Michael Fishbane and Joanna Weinberg. Oxford: The Littman Library of Jewish Civilization, 2013.

Moore, Thomas. *Care of the Soul.* New York: HarperCollins, 1992.

Mysticism and Sacred Scripture. Edited by Steven T. Katz. Oxford: Oxford University Press, 2000.

Ouaknin, Marc-Alain. *The Burnt Book.* Translated by Llewellyn Brown. Princeton: Princeton University Press, 1995.

Ricoeur, Paul. "The Bible and the Imagination." In *The Bible as a Document of the University,* edited by H. D. Betz, 49–75. Chico, CA: Scholars, 1981.

Sarna, Nahum. *Exploring Exodus: The Heritage of Biblical Israel.* New York: Schocken, 1986.

Scholem, Gershom. *Kabbalah.* New York: Meridian Books, New American Library, 1978.

———. *Major Trends of Jewish Mysticism.* New York: Schocken, 1941.

———. *On the Kabbalah and its Symbolism.* Translated by R. Manheim. New York: Schocken, 1965.

Silver, Daniel Jeremy. *Images of Moses.* New York: Basic, 1982.

———. *Sabbatai Sevi: The Mystical Messiah.* Translated by R. J. Zwi Werblowsky. Bollingen Series XCIII. Princeton, NJ: Princeton University Press, 1973.

Spiegel, Shalom. *The Last Trial, On the Legends and Lord of the Command to Abraham to Offer Isaac as a Sacrifice: the Akedah.* Translated by Judah Goldin. New York: Schocken, 1967.

Strenski, Ivan. *Theology and the First Theory of Sacrifice.* Brill: Leiden. 2003.

Strouma, Guy G. *The End of Sacrifice: Religious Transformations in Late Antiquity.* Translated by Susan Emanuel. Chicago: University of Chicago Press, 2009.

Tishby, Isaiah. *Messianic Mysticism: Moses Hayim Luzzatto and the Padua School.* Oxford: The Littman Library of Jewish Civilization, 2008.

Wellek, Rene, and Austin Warren. *Theory of Literature.* New York: Harcourt, Brace, 1949.

Wineman, Aryeh. *The Hasidic Parable.* Philadelphia: Jewish Publication Society, 2001.

———. "Hewn from the Divine Quarry: An Analysis of Yitzhak of Radvil's *Or Yitzhak.*" *Hebrew Union College Annual* 77 (2006) 179–207.

———. "How the Hasidic Masters Read the Torah." *Conservative Judaism* 60.1–2 (2007–8) 62–73.

———. *Letters of Light, Passages from Ma'or va-shemesh.* Eugene, OR: Wipf and Stock, 2015.

———. "Sufis in the Hasidic *Mishkan.*" *Conservative Judaism* 64.4 (2013) 110–20.

———. "A Wrestling with Interpretation in a Classical Hasidic Text." *Conservative Judaism* 49:2 (1997) 68–74.

CPSIA information can be obtained
at www.ICGtesting.com
Printed in the USA
FSHW020707100419
57110FS